Can I Pray for You?

An Unexpected Meeting between a Chicagoan Oncologist and God

YOUNG KWANG CHAE

And hope does not put us to shame, because God's love has been poured out into our hearts through the Holy Spirit, who has been given to us.

~ Romans 5:5 NIV ~

Scripture quotations marked NIV are taken from the *Holy Bible, New International Version*®, NIV®. Copyright © 1973, 1978, 1984, 2011 by Biblica, Inc.™ Used by permission of Zondervan. All rights reserved worldwide. www.zondervan.com. The "NIV" and "New International Version" are trademarks registered in the United States Patent and Trademark Office by Biblica, Inc.™

Scripture quotations marked KJV are taken from the *King James Version* of the Bible. Public domain.

Scripture quotations marked AMP are taken from the *AMPLIFIED® BIBLE*, Copyright© 1954, 1958, 1962, 1964, 1965, 1987 by the Lockman Foundation Used by Permission. (www.Lockman.org)

Scripture quotations marked NET are taken from the *NET Bible*® copyright © 1996, 2019 by Biblical Studies Press, L.L.C. https://netbible.com All rights reserved.

Scripture quotations marked NASB are taken from the *New American Standard Bible*®, Copyright © 1960, 1962, 1963, 1968, 1971, 1972, 1973, 1975, 1977, 1995 by The Lockman Foundation. Used by permission.

Scripture quotations marked NLT are taken from the *Holy Bible, New Living Translation*, copyright © 1996, 2004, 2015 by Tyndale House Foundation. Used by permission of Tyndale House Publishers, Carol Stream, Illinois 60188. All rights reserved.

Scripture quotations marked JUB are taken *Jubilee Bible 2000*. Copyright © 2013, 2020 by Ransom Press International.

Can I Pray for You?
ISBN: 978-1-685730-46-8
Copyright © 2024 by Young Kwang Chae

Published by Word and Spirit Publishing
P.O. Box 701403
Tulsa, Oklahoma 74170
wordandspiritpublishing.com

Printed in the United States of America. All rights reserved under International Copyright Law. Content and/or cover may not be reproduced in whole or in part in any form without the expressed written consent of the Publisher.

This book is dedicated to

my biggest supporter, my helping hand,

and the Giving Tree in my life:

my late father-in-law

(Eek June Chung)

Translated by

Sung Mi Yoon, Cyra Yoonsun Kang, Liam Il Young Chung, Jewel Park, Grace Lee, Alice Lee, Cecilia Jimyung Nam, Soowon Lee, Hye Sung Kim

Edited by

Yunjoo Lee, Emma Jae Young Yu, Ilene Hong, Jennifer Sebin Bok, Joo Hee Park, Min Jeong Kim, Leeseul Kim, Sally Chan Mi Jung, Youjin Oh, Lena Chae, Hae In Chung, Liam Il Young Chung, Hye Sung Kim

Contents

Endorsements — ix

Prologue: When God Pours His Love — xvii

Part I: **That Day, When I Had No Love in Me** — 1

    Can I Pray for You? — 3

    I Had No Love to Give My Mentees — 13

    Strongly Believing That I Was Right — 17

    Keyword 1
    Friend: confessing that I had no love in me — 21

Part II: **The Things I Started Seeing after Learning to Love** — 25

    I Found Honor in My Name — 27

    Becoming a Novice Coordinator — 37

    Keyword 2
    Direction: learning from the heart of the vineyard owner — 41

    A Surprise Gift from Morning Prayers — 44

    Everything Led Up to This Moment — 49

The End of the Earth Is under My Feet — 53

Words I Want to Hear from God — 61

Keyword 3
Scars: my scars are my talents — 66

Part III: God's Words of Love toward Students — 69

Perfect Timing — 71

Young Kwang, I Entrust Them in Your Care — 76

Keyword 4
Listening: ministry begins with listening — 82

Unexpected Proposal:
Ten-Minute Morning Prayer — 85

Unexpected Proposal: Morning Book Club — 89

A Cameo Life Starring Friendship — 93

Keyword 5
Celebration: a sense of encouragement
and recognition — 98

Ongoing Relay of Testimonies in the Lab — 101

An All-Line That Doesn't Sleep — 104

Even Make Academic Conference
Trips Different — 108

Keyword 6
Character: a good teacher is seen in life — 111

Part IV: **God's Words of Love toward Patients** — 113

A Patient's Prayer That Teared Me Up — 115

Can I Pray for You? — 118

Every Moment Is God's Work — 121

Keyword 7
Empathy: listen and listen with your heart — 124

Albert's Tears — 127

You Are My Priority — 132

Rounds Include Family, Too — 138

Keyword 8
Best: one who is more sincere than I — 146

Research Begins with Love for Patients — 149

Part V: **To My Patients Who Are Doing Well** — 155

May I Come In? — 157

It's Not Your Fault — 161

Miracles Begin Once You Let Go of Numbers — 164

Keyword 9
Acceptance: there is no miracle on the cross — 169

Together through Mourning and Hope — 172

I Will Be with You until the End — 179

Part VI: **Revival Already Underway** — 187

One Who Heals Friendships — 189

Living Like I'm the Last Christian — 197

Keyword 10
Obedience: the spiritual Ohm's law — 204

The Beginning of Mission — 207

Go and Do Likewise — 213

Dreaming of the Grapevine Ministry — 221

Epilogue: Dreaming of a Strange Vineyard — 227

Endorsements

What does it mean to be a "Christian doctor?" How can we express our faith through our work to transform it into a genuine calling? This is a difficult but crucial question that must be answered by everyone who follows Jesus. It is a difficult question because while the church may provide general guidelines of discipleship, we will need to discover in very personal ways how to live out these kingdom values in the unique circumstances to which we've been called. It is a crucial question because most of our waking hours will be spent in our places of work. If we cannot live out our faith there, then a huge opportunity to shine the light of Jesus is lost.

As a medical doctor, I deeply resonated with Dr. Chae's experiences throughout this book. I remember my own initial nervousness when I first gathered the courage to pray with a patient. His accounts of living out his faith as a physician are inspiring, demonstrating how God used each step of faith and obedience to impact the lives of countless patients and colleagues. Dr. Chae shares not only his successes but also his challenges and setbacks. His humility reminds us that we are all imperfect vessels and works-in-progress. These candid confessions give us hope that God works through us despite our weaknesses.

As Dr. Chae's pastor, I've had the privilege of witnessing firsthand the authenticity of his faith and his desire to live meaningfully in God's eyes. He has often approached me after Sunday services seeking prayer for his challenges or new opportunities, embodying the truth that we can do nothing without Jesus. Having spoken several times to his Grapevine Ministry, I've observed the profound influence he has on his colleagues. Reading this book has personally challenged and inspired me to reflect on how God might work through me in this season of my life. I believe you will find it equally inspiring.

—**Senior pastor Steve Lee** of Immanuel Community Church

This is a unique and extraordinary book! It not only provides a great deal of spiritual wisdom, truth, and insight, but also shows a great example of how one might live as a Christian disciple today at the workplace. Written by Dr. Young Kwang Chae, a research oncologist in Chicago and a committed Christ follower, this book provides testimony after testimony and wisdom after wisdom, weaving together real, everyday encounters with God and people met while working as a medical professional. Dr. Chae is a brilliant doctor and researcher. He is a renowned expert in his field. What is more remarkable, however, is how he has learned throughout his journey as a disciple of Jesus over the years and practices daily the integration of his spiritual life with his professional life. He lives them out never as two separate things but one, just as the Bible tells us. That is how biblical characters such as Abraham, David, Daniel, Nehemiah, and Paul lived their lives—faith and work integrated as one.

Dr. Chae's life as a research doctor involves not only professionalism but also prayer, listening to God, and loving patients as Jesus would. He prioritizes treating people with love and care and building relationships. This book has many stories from hospitals and labs due to his everyday life setting, but they may not be so different from stories from a restaurant, school, farm, or bank. While this book would encourage medical professionals, it is not only for them. This book would inspire all Christ followers who want to integrate their faith with their work and live a missional and missionary life.

—**Peter T. Lee**, Faculty Member of Trinity Evangelical Divinity School; Missiologist of Operation Mobilization

In the high school student group at Abjection Church, there was a brother named Soohyun Ahn. Like Jesus, he went to heaven at the young age of thirty-three. He was truly a remarkable Christian doctor who resembled Jesus. Whenever I see Dr. Chae Young-Gwang at Chicago's Northwestern University Hospital, I can't help but think that he resembles the 'foolish doctor' An Soo Hyun. Dr. Chae's newly published book, *Can I Pray for You?*, took me back to when I read *A Foolish Doctor*. It is truly a blessing that such wonderful Christian doctors continue to emerge.

—**Pastor Dong Ho Kim**, head of the Ezekiel Missions

It has been a while since I read *Finding God in Unexpected Places* by the Christian writer Philip Yancey, but the book still gives me the same feelings. Through that book, he testifies to the amazing works of God in places where human thoughts and hearts cannot expect, and he vividly portrays the fingerprints of God's hand deeply engraved in those places. Meeting Professor Chae and witnessing what is happening in his research lab in downtown Chicago was undoubtedly God's work that made my heart beat faster. It was another living testimony to *Finding God in Unexpected Places*.

I remember a Korean doctor who was working diligently, researching in a lab and seeing patients in a clinic. He did not believe in God while he was in Korea working his way toward his American dream. When he was searching for jobs in America, he was introduced to Dr. Chae, who was well-known in the Korean community for helping Korean doctors secure physician jobs in the United States. When I met up with the doctor later on, he said, "After working with Professor Chae for a while, I've realized that although I don't know much about religions or God, if this is the God that Dr. Chae believes in, then I should think about it deeply." A few weeks later, he accepted God as his Savior. Two weeks after that, he prayed as such:

"Hello, Father God. I am XX. God, if I can serve You better, please give me trials . . ."

Because Dr. Chae envisions a future where his disciples are more successful than him, Dr. Chae, who serves his students with all his heart, is a Christian doctor who has received love and tears for patients and their families as a gift from Jesus. I am overjoyed for the publication of this book that records and testifies to the work of God in Dr. Chae's research lab. I believe this book is just the beginning. I eagerly anticipate the arrival of God's Kingdom in various medical fields through Northwestern University Hospital and his disciples.

—**Tae Hoon Kim**, Ethiopian missionary

Life's battlefield is intense. Living as a disciple can be confusing beyond the intensity. That's why I received many questions when I was in ministry, such as, "So, how should we live?" Even if there was awe after listening to sermons, the subsequent sense of alienation and confusion would have been inevitable for those who tried to live by faith alone. They may not sufficiently address the confusion faced by those trying to live by faith alone.

To me, Dr. Young Kwang Chae's book was like a refreshing rain after a drought. This book did not approach theological issues related to the holistic Christian life logically, nor did it provide principles that everyone should apply. Nevertheless, it seems to deal with the problems that many people are struggling with and offer direction. It speaks not about how to live, but about the attitude with which to live, and not simply about what happened, but about the heart with which it happened. Rather than recommending this book, I am convinced that it will serve as a refreshing rain to quench the thirst of everyone living by faith. Instead of recommending this book, I recommend the life of Dr. Young Kwang Chae, the author of this book.

—**Pastor Jin-Joon Roh**, head of the Preaching Coaching Ministry

This book is a narrative of faith that involves creating people with God's love, realizing their calling during this journey, and living a zealous missional life. As someone who has worked as a missionary for a long time, I often wondered how to live a missional life, which has become a lifelong question. This book also serves as a missional mobilization letter that provides practical proposals and answers on how to live a missional life. As the author says, "A missional life is a life that comes to life naturally when you obey and rely on God," and it is a life that "pays forward" rather than "pays back." I deeply agree with the profound missional reflection that he presents, and it has given me a new perspective.

Personally, as a senior colleague to the late Dr. Soohyun Ahn, the author of *The Foolish Young Doctor*, during our time at medical school, I often think that if Dr. Ahn were still alive, he would be living a life similar to Dr. Chae's today. Dr. Chae serves our lives in the field of our everyday existence, making our lives richer with his extraordinary missional spirit, just like *The Foolish Young Doctor*. Reading this book, I hope that all readers will be filled with God's heart and discover their mission in missional life. When God's heart deepens and expands, we will all become reflections of the Lord, glorifying Him.

—**Kwan Tae Park**, past director of Mongolian Agape Hospital, transplant surgeon

"Can I come in?" As Dr. Chae knocks on the door to the treatment room, he prays: *May God reach the mind and body of this patient, may God allow me to treat this patient with love and compassion.* A clinic appointment that begins with a prayer sometimes leads to the courage to ask, "Can I pray for you, too?" Such small acts of courage reveal the amazing and significant events that God has worked through this book.

A renowned figure in the field of oncology, recognized by the medical community and global media, he is sought after by aspiring students worldwide. However, what we really want to know from him is his faith. The book's impact lies in the fact that the faith he speaks of is not an abstract concept but a life lived and a life connected. He views medicine "not merely as a technology but as an art of building relationships."

I recommend this book to not only doctors, but also to those who serve and care for people, and to all who wish to enrich the lives of others with what they have. It will provide comfort and hope to those who are battling scary and tiresome diseases, including cancer, and their families. If you are someone interested in how the power of faith can change real-life situations, you will find this book's challenges unforgettable. For attentive readers, you will sense the voice asking, "May I come in?" as the love of the Lord approaches you, and you will experience the grace of meeting Him deeply.

—**Senior pastor Young-Ho Park** of Pohang Jeil Church

I am delighted to see a book about the missional life of a medical professional who holds on to God's time, even in everyday life. After I talked with Dr. Chae about writing a testimonial for his book, I pulled up a photo from his wedding where I served as the officiant. I remember seeing a burning passion behind his bright eyes. Through his book, I have reunited with Dr. Chae after all these years, and I am proud to say that he is still the mature disciple living diligently to resemble God.

Dr. Chae lives a life that is consistent within and outside the Church. He sets a good example for those who tend to separate faith from their world and fail to take action. The confessions of Dr. Chae, who is at once a doctor, a professor, and a father, will deeply resonate with readers.

The author's insight and practical advice contained in each page of the book will inspire change in the lives of those who wish to live a true Christian life.

—**Senior pastor Jung-Hyun Oh** of Sarang Church

It's refreshing to read a book written by someone who truly believes in Jesus. Professor Chae graduated from Seoul National University College of Medicine and passed the board exam as an oncologist in America. He now treats patients as a professor of oncology at Northwestern University Memorial Hospital in Chicago and annually serves as a mentor and lecturer in KOSTA USA.

While he has achieved significant academic success, Dr. Chae wants to be recognized for his faith. His faith is not abstract; he is not just shouting from the pulpit—he writes about his real life experiences. As a result, Dr. Chae's community in Chicago is experiencing a revival of faith.

This book includes stories of how God has led Dr. Chae to his work at Northwestern University, the happenings in his clinic and laboratory, the loving relationships between cancer patients and their caregivers, and the prayers, laughter, tears, and dreams discussed in the weekly morning book clubs and weekly testimony meetings.

In particular, the COVID-19 pandemic has deepened his wisdom. Reading this book felt like seeing another "foolish doctor" like Soohyun Ahn, resembling the Lord in the way he sincerely treats all his patients with love. I was very happy to meet someone with such spiritual vigor and profound understanding of God's world, someone who is truly the child of Jesus.

Professor Young Kwant Chae honestly reflects on himself in this book, allowing readers to measure his faith and learn about how God is working through him. I hope readers themselves have a chance to discover God's work in their lives. It is the author's intention that his book would act as a guide to a Christian lifestyle for health-care providers, a source of consolation for patients and their families, and above all, an answer to the prayers of young Christians and international students who are scared and confused in this world.

—**Senior pastor Gi-Sung Yoo**, Good Shepherd Church

The book details the story of a doctor who lives a missionary life even in the workplace. I am thrilled that the book has been released to the world. The author shows us through his life experiences and lifestyle that love can be present in the most painful experiences. His stories of love testify that wherever Christ's love reaches can be truly united and restored. I was very touched by the way love has affected the lives of terminal cancer patients and their families. I highly recommend this book to all professionals and believers who dream of the Kingdom of God in their respective positions and want to learn about the life of a missional life.

—**Sang-Hyuk Yoon**, Department of Rehabilitative Medicine at Pyongyang College of Medicine

When I met Professor Chae at Bethel Church in Baltimore, my first impression was that he was a very "true and clear young man." In this book, I am seeing another side of Dr. Chae, a doctor who cries and prays for his patients, mentors young disciples, leads book clubs, and above all, serves as the Lord's disciple, spiritual leader, and outstanding specialist in cancer treatment who uses the clinic as a mission field. I read this book in its entirety in one sitting; I have felt challenged every day since. I would like to learn from him and become more similar to the Lord's true disciples, who sincerely want to be filled with God's love and truly wish for the success of others. I hope you are able to finish this journey to the very end.

—**Pastor Soon-Geun Lee**, Da Ae Church

People outside the Church are able to recognize whether people within the Church are real Christians or not. They observe the ways Christians lead their lives and judge whether Christians are any different from them. Although the author is a recognized oncologist, his faith is of the utmost importance to God. Through this "strange doctor" who strives to teach the real meaning and importance to his patients, teachers, and coworkers, God asks us: "Who do you want to be recognized by? What are you working for?" To a world that values success and happiness, the story about a "strange Christian" can make a lasting impact. I sincerely recommend this book, as it pushes us to reach our potential to change the world.

—**Senior pastor Chan-Soo Lee**, Bundang Woori Church

Not all Christians are able to become missionaries, but all Christians should live a missional life. Unfortunately, most of them actually live like Monday atheists, living a life that is nothing like explained in the gospel once they leave the walls of the church.

Professor Young Kwang Chae is the epitome of what it means to live a missional life. Not only did he graduate from Seoul National University College of Medicine and accomplish many great things as an oncologist in America, he also prays and provides words of wisdom to patients as a Christian missionary. Through his prayers and words, he is the light to patients suffering from cancer. On top of that, he spends every morning teaching Christian values to doctors and students in his lab.

I am so grateful to see this book inspire us to follow the example of Christ, living a life that includes church, family, career, and faith.

—**Heart surgeon Soo-Young Peter Chung**, president of GMMA

While living in an unrighteous and depraved era, Christians constantly ask, "Lord, where on earth are You? What are You doing?" This book is an answer to these questions. "While you are busily living without love, I am pouring love to those who are desperately asking for My love." Author Young Kwang Chae works every day in his lab and clinic, as well as in his family, touching all with love. As a result, I realize that wherever he stands is the end of the earth.

Jesus commands discipleship to His children who have forgotten about their first love. While reading this book, those who have ears will surely hear His name.

—**Senior pastor Jungmin Cho**, BASIC Church

Prologue

When God Pours His Love

In November 2020, when the COVID-19 pandemic remained a grave threat in the United States, my oldest daughter had to stay home and attend classes virtually. I felt sorry for my daughter, who was having such a hard time not being able to take even a single step out of the house or see her friends at school. I decided to bring her to my office every morning so she could at least get some fresh air.

While I was taking care of my patients in the clinic, my daughter took online classes in my office. It didn't take long until my daughter started talking to the interns and students in my lab and getting closer to them. Then, one day my daughter told me that she also wanted to participate in the prayer and book club activities that I led for my students and interns every morning. The moment I heard those words, I was both touched and elated. After we started doing these activities together, she began to appreciate hearing stories and sharing new experiences with my students.

Can I Pray for You?

One day while I was talking with my daughter in bed, she told me: "Dad, I was surprised that you were committed to these kinds of ministries [the book club and prayer meetings]. I'm sorry that I ignored you for the past few years ... I'm so proud of you, Dad."

In fact, ever since my daughter hit puberty, my relationship with her had not been the same. But since that night, reestablishing a better relationship with her became one of my main prayer requests. I did not expect that the COVID-19 pandemic would be a blessing in disguise. God answered my prayers when I least expected it.

In that moment, I could "feel" the true love of God entering my heart. God has transformed me from a "selfish, immature being" into a true "human being" who understands the value of love and faith. Upon that realization, I wanted to boast about the path I had walked with God. I wanted to witness the love and greatness of God, who called me as a tool to treat and cure cancer patients and teach students at a university hospital in the United States. I wanted to record the stories of my life—the stories that only God and I shared—for my three lovely children and my students.

When I moved to the United States in 2005, after finishing medical school and my mandatory military service in Korea, I worked and studied tirelessly as I was determined to achieve my goals. Currently, I am in charge of treating cancer patients and teaching students at Northwestern Memorial Hospital in Chicago. As the co-director of the Clinical Trials Center, I am conducting multiple projects related

Prologue: When God Pours His Love

to the development of new drugs and clinical trial-related studies. In collaboration with the U.S. government, I also lead nationwide clinical trials related to precision medicine and immunotherapy.

Most of my patients tell me that I am their "last hope," claiming they have tried every single treatment option—to no avail. Of course, when I manage to provide them with medical support, I experience tremendous joy and fulfillment. However, I also feel great joy and happiness when I know that I can sympathize with them and accompany them on their challenging journey even if the treatments don't work on them. I gain a sense of fulfillment from the fact that I can laugh and cry together with my patients.

During my journey with patients, God provided valuable disciples to me: my students. After realizing that something ordinary or trivial to me can be extraordinary for someone, or even be a "special gift from God," or the Holy Spirit working within them, I wanted to testify that God is alive, as well as help them also to witness the greatness of God for themselves.

In fact, I witnessed the work of God while hosting book clubs and testimony sessions with my students. For years, I started my medical practice at 8 A.M. Every day. At 6:40 A.M., before starting the clinic, I gathered my menttees, prayed together for ten minutes, and then began a book club meeting. Around November 2019, I also began mentoring a group of undergraduate students at Northwestern University who wished to join my book club.

However, Northwestern University is located in a city called Evanston, a thirty-minute drive away from the northern part of Chicago. In addition to that, there were no shuttle buses from the school to the hospital before 8 a.m., so I suggested that the students participate in the book club virtually. Since then, most of the ministries of my lab naturally began to take place virtually.

In April 2020, as the number of COVID-19 cases peaked in the United States, having face-to-face meetings became nearly impossible. Thankfully, our lab was still able to continue online meetings to share God's wisdom and the grace that He has poured out on our lives. Also, since most of the alumni from my lab came from many different countries and cities, I felt that a new platform was being established where all alumni and mentors interested in my work could participate freely without any restrictions of time and space. I came to think that I should document the stories of my own and my students' testimonies through my online/offline ministries.

In October of that same year, Dr. Tae-hoon Kim, a missionary who has been serving in Ethiopia for years, was on sabbatical in Los Angeles, California, and he had the chance to visit my lab. After spending a few days with my lab workers, he suggested that I should write a book about my experience with the ministry over the past years. At first, I felt a bit embarrassed because I did not believe what I had done was something that deserves much praise. I thought

Prologue: When God Pours His Love

there were many devout Christian doctors out there who were doing similar work as mine.

However, as I was praying, I felt that God was doing great things in my lab and clinic in Chicago. Then I was moved to leave a piece of my journey with God and how He has been faithfully working in my lab and clinic. After wrestling with it for a while, I decided to obey His will.

Ever since I made the decision, I began to realize that I was truly blessed with many exemplary books. When I first read the book *That Young Foolish Doctor*, I was thrilled to realize how faith can harmoniously be applied in a professional setting. I thought my testimony might allow me to pay back the wandering souls who were struggling to find their faith and true purpose in life, just like I did in the past. This was when frustration and embarrassment gradually disappeared, and rather, new hopes and expectations began to fill up my heart.

This book has been written for those who want to experience the presence of God. In particular, it is written for those who are curious about how faith and medicine, faith and practice, can be synchronously applied in real-life settings. I hope this book serves as sound guidance for medical students—or any students who wish to work anywhere in the field of medicine—who feel lost and do not have a mentor. I also want this book to be a source of comfort, hope, and encouragement for patients and their families, especially those who have been scarred and hurt by doctors in the past. Last but not least, I hope this book is a "response" to someone's unanswered prayer.

I would like to express my deepest gratitude to my one and only soul mate, my beautiful wife, Rachel Haein Chung; my three lovely children, Lena, Nathan, and Emily; my parents; my father-in-law, my mother-in-law; my younger sister; my brother-in-law and his wife; and the faithful mentors and members of my Grapevine Ministry Team.

I would also like to thank my students, colleagues, and patients who have allowed me to share their stories throughout this book.

Finally, I would like to start by offering you "A Cup of Tea" and invite you to learn the story of my life.

A Cup of Tea

by
Young Kwang Chae

Would you like
A cup of tea?

I pour boiling water dyed in the color of rose
Brewing the clear, crisp autumn lake
A spoonful of warm hug
Two spoonfuls of comforting gaze
Three spoonfuls of words of encouragement
Pour it into a sturdy, yet humble teacup
Then stir.
Stir . . . stir . . . stir . . .

For eternal happiness
That will eventually prevail
Placing a petal of marigold

A cup of tea
Just for you
You are welcome here
Again and always.

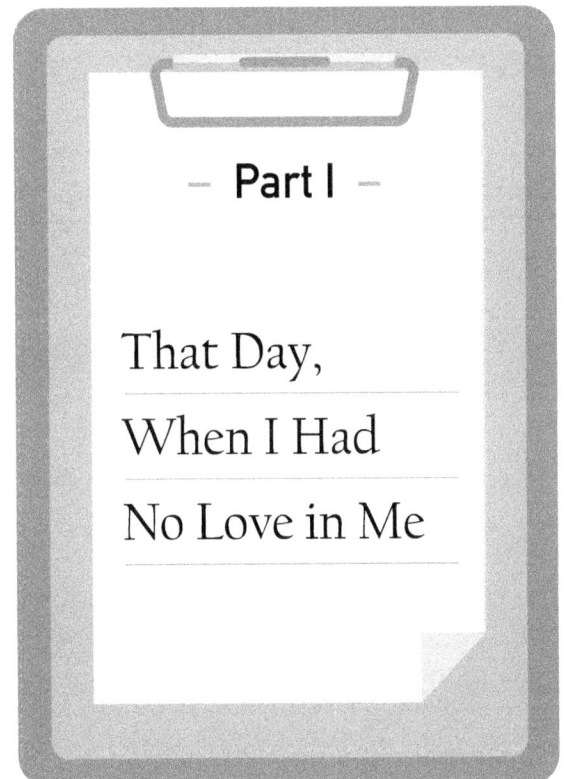

Part I

That Day, When I Had No Love in Me

Can I Pray for You?

Meeting Those Who Are Hungry for Love

After the COVID-19 pandemic, I spent a significant amount of time online or on the phone, because it was so difficult to meet my patients face-to-face. Virtual visits caused a great deal of stress for me; it was more tiring to understand the patient's condition or what they were trying to express without nonverbal communication.

One day, one of my patients unexpectedly asked me at the end of our call if I could pray for him. I was a bit flustered, as I was in a conference room with other doctors and nurses. However, I collected myself and prayed for the patient, asking God to bless this man with His grace and for his quick recovery.

After a few days, during my daily hospital rounds, another of my patients also said to me, "I would really appreciate it if you could pray for me." I was surprised by the sudden request once again. However, I held her hand and prayed for her without hesitation, asking for God's blessing.

Can I Pray for You?

After experiencing these two series of events, I asked God, "Why is this happening to me? What are You trying to tell me?" In the past, God came to my heart and nudged me as I was treating my patients. Whenever this happened, I would normally initiate by asking the patients, "Can I pray for you?" And every time I prayed for my patients, I could feel God was showering His love to me for my patients. Sometimes His love was so great that it made me burst into tears. However, there had never been a case when patients had asked me to pray for them first.

One morning, when I was driving on the highway to work, God spoke to me by saying, "Do you know why they approached you first, My son? Can't you love your patients a little more? They are all My precious children."

That was when I realized so clearly that my heart was still too feeble and empty to understand His infinite love. So, I answered God, "You are right. There was no love in me. I'm sorry. I am so sorry."

My eyes watered as I felt my sincere remorse before the Lord. After weeping in tears for some time, I prayed again: "Father, please fill me with Your overflowing and endless love. And help me to pour out Your love onto my patients." My eyes were so blurry with tears I was shedding that I even thought about pulling over on the highway.

So, ever since that morning, during my daily prayers I felt so overwhelmed by His love and mercy that I wasn't able to fight back tears.

Can I Pray for You?

God's Love Surpasses All Understanding

I could feel that I was being transformed. I started saying, "I support you. I love you," to my patients without feeling shy or hesitant. Even in the United States, it can be quite awkward for doctors to express their "love" toward their patients. But after God so dramatically poured out His love into me, each patient of mine became more important and precious to me. I was able to understand them and put myself in their shoes. It naturally became easier for me to say the words like "I'm sorry" or "I love you." When I realized that I truly am nothing without His grace and mercy, I was amazed and grateful by the fact that God has blessed me to look after patients here in the clinic—and each of them is a child of His.

One day I found myself tearing up after every patient encounter. When I was crying all day in my office, my patients came up to me and expressed their gratitude by saying, "You are my lifesaver and my angel." I was so grateful for my patients. My reverence toward God, who is worthy of all the praise, grew bigger as I was able to feel His love and grace even more.

Another change within myself was that I became more compassionate and sensitive to even the smallest troubles that bothered them. One time, an old woman came up to me and said that she had been suffering from dry mouth, nausea, and insomnia related to her recent treatments, and these eventually caused her to be hospitalized. I wanted to buy this patient a unique type of gum that attaches to the roof of the mouth; I remembered one patient telling me that this gum helped to stimulate saliva production. After finishing my schedule at the office, I bought the gum and swung by her hospital room. She was very pleased to see me. It was quite sad to see her, though, because she could barely move due to her worsening condition. It was apparent that she did not have much time left.

I believe it is so meaningful to spend our last days on earth with friends and family members, looking back on our lives. Patients with terminal disease have an option for hospice care, a treatment plan that focuses on relieving pain and suffering instead of pursuing further treatment with a curative intent so that patients can die peacefully. For patients who have less than six months left to live and are candidates for hospice care, I usually initiate a conversation about their relationships with family members and other loved ones.

When I explained hospice care to this woman and offered the option, the patient answered, "Yes." I also asked her whether she was at peace with God. She responded that she used to go to church, but later in her life, after studying other theories and philosophies, she determined that Jesus was only a human being, not God Himself. She then began to talk to me for a long time about her beliefs and her life.

To be honest, I was a bit surprised and frustrated by her reaction, because I had never hear a patient answer my question like this before. It felt as if some part of my mind was telling me that I should not have asked that kind of question. For a moment, I wanted to finish the conversation as quickly as possible. But when I looked back at her peaceful face, the name *Jesus* and a verse from the book of Acts came to mind:

> "Neither is there salvation in any other: for there is none other name under heaven given among men, whereby we must be saved."
> —ACTS 4:12 KJV

Once she finished with her story, I said, "Thank you for sharing your thoughts with me in such detail. I just wanted to tell you one thing: I'm confident that the name of Jesus has the power of salvation. I love you. That is why I want to give you the best I can."

She listened to me, stared into my eyes for a few moments, and then said, "I love it that you love me."

After that moment, her heart was wide open toward Jesus. Our conversation went even further as she began to confess Jesus as her Lord and Savior. It was something that I didn't expect to happen—but it was a moment of salvation. This moment filled my heart with joy, happiness, and gratitude. To me, this became a proof of God teaching me that "love" can transcend and exist beyond all human logic. In that moment, I realized the unexpected outpouring of emotions I'd had while driving on the highway was part of God's great plan to prepare me for this beautiful moment of salvation. I was so happy to experience the Holy Spirit working within me—one who had lacked such love.

This experience reminded me of one patient who said, "I love you," even before I did. This patient was a young father of two lovely children. None of the existing treatment methods available had worked for him. He had decided to try various clinical trials and novel treatments with me, but he ended up in the emergency room due to a severe case of sepsis. When I heard that I was hospitalized, my nurse and I rushed out of the clinic and headed to the ER, thinking this might be our last time with the patient. Despite his worsening condition, the patient maintained a clear sense of consciousness.

When I saw him, he looked me straight in the eye as he said the words, "Thank you," and "I love you." He told us that he was happy and wanted to thank us for walking together with him on his long and difficult journey.

The patient had loved me first, even before I had loved him. At that moment, a verse from the book of 1 John echoed in my mind:

> In this is love, not that we loved God, but that He loved us.
> —1 John 4:10 AMP

I felt it was time for me to return the love I received from my patients.

The Fruit of Faith Is Patience, Not Success

Expressing love to my patients has helped me realize the importance of accompanying them as they endure the difficult treatment process. For several years, my clinic team and I gave awards to patients who successfully completed the treatment process or had undergone treatment for a long time. To those on the last day of a twelve-week chemotherapy regimen following lung cancer treatment, we awarded a certificate of "chemotherapy completion"; to the few patients on the one-hundredth cycle of immunotherapy, we presented a milestone certificate of "one-hundredth immunotherapy." We would visit patients at the infusion center and celebrate as if we were hosting a birthday party. These events provided great joy and memories to patients, as well as everyone on our medical team.

However, I quickly realized these celebrations can have great contradictions. The shift of thought was from a patient who was a mother of two college-aged children. Her disease had failed to respond to every possible treatment option, which included chemotherapy, targeted therapy, immunotherapy, and even clinical trials. I always faced this patient with a heavy heart. One day, we saw that a new combination therapy appeared to have decreased the size of her tumor; she even regained enough strength to go on a short vacation with her family. We were hopeful as we planned to create an award to celebrate her first response to treatment. What followed, however, was devastating news: her follow-up CT scan showed metastasis to other organs of her body. I was hit hard by this news; I felt very sorry and saddened that I could not encourage the patient with a new event.

Amid this flurry of emotions, I reflected on the situation and came upon a new realization: I do not only have to celebrate the "successes" in a patient's journey through treatment. Rather than focusing solely on "results," I can always celebrate and recognize a patient's "attitude" and "spirit." With this, I started praying to God and found myself apologizing before Him again. I realized I had gotten used to recognizing and remembering only the success stories in life; as a consequence, I had forgotten about the value of patience and persistence. I had overlooked the beauty of patience that arises from continuous struggle. I had forgotten the beauty of a smile that persists through difficult times.

As reflected in Hebrews 12:1 (NET), one of the missions God has given us in life is to "run with endurance the race set out for us." To complete this race, we are set out to go through all sorts of paths, narrow and wide. In passing through the valleys, we may encounter the devastating news of a cancer diagnosis or the failure to respond to cancer therapies. However, we must still push forward and look forward to the day when we complete the race of faith; at some point during or at the end of the race, God rewards us.

For these reasons, I came up with a new award: the award of endurance. My team and I presented it to the patient above, along with two other patients who had not been responding to any of their treatments. All the patients told us that this award was a huge source of encouragement to them. As they expressed their joy with tears in their eyes, my team and I stood with them, sharing in their happiness. In a place where there seemed to be no hope, God allowed us the opportunity to celebrate and be happy together. My team and I learned we can encourage patients not only with "results," but also for their positive "attitude" through this precious opportunity.

Above all, this was an opportunity to vividly realize what kind of comfort and encouragement comes to patients when God's love is poured out.

The story does not end here. The day we held these celebrations, none of those three patients experienced an improvement in their symptoms, neither did their CT results show any positive news. But as we refocused our attention to loving our patients, God gave them not only joy in their hearts, but also the courage to endure. Through this, I was able to feel God's heart more deeply for us who are suffering—that is, for the sick.

God never enjoys our suffering. He is Someone who can relate to all our pain. With His love, we can encourage, bless, and celebrate each other's journeys, no matter how dark they may be. Jesus said, "But seek ye first the kingdom of God, and his righteousness; and all these things shall be added unto you" (Matthew 6:33 KJV). I believe that if we all sought after the Kingdom of God by loving each other, we would be simultaneously gifted with recovery and salvation.

I know myself very well. In and of myself, I do not possess much love. I especially lack empathy. Therefore, I always go before the Lord with a feeble heart. Without the Lord, there is no hope, so I humbly go to the place of prayer to find hope in the time of need. God knows this side of me, so He showers me with love. And armed with His love, I find myself loving my patients so much more than I could on my own.

> In your relationships with one another, have the same mindset as Christ Jesus.
> —Philippians 2:5 NIV

I believe that when this "mindset as Christ Jesus" is given to us, God's recovery and salvation will be declared in our bodies and spirits.

I Had No Love to Give My Mentees

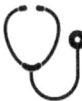

God's Love Poured into the Lab

The day I cried on the highway and in the clinic after experiencing the Holy Spirit is a day I struggle to comprehend even now.

What happened that day prompted a change in how I view not only my patients, but also my mentees. Up until that point, I had prided myself in how well I took care of my mentees. Not only did I help them academically, but I also tried my best to guide them spiritually by planning book clubs and other similar activities for them. That specific morning, however, God helped me to see how earnestly my mentees were working to prepare for their residency interviews. Every year around late fall, the majority of my mentees would apply for residency or fellowship programs and interview for a position in the United States. Their journey was predictable to me, as I had also had to go through the same process multiple times to get to where I was.

Can I Pray for You?

It finally occurred to me that I did not possess much love inside me. Even as I observed my mentees working hard and helping each other prepare for their interviews, I never once thought of giving them a hand. As a faculty member at a university hospital here in the States, I would participate as an interviewer when selecting medical students, residents, and full-time doctors, so I knew how to approach the interview as a good candidate. But even with this knowledge, I had failed to help my mentees when they needed it the most.

However, on that day, while running the research lab, I was infinitely ashamed of myself, one who had thought *Let's make others succeed* was my motto. Having suddenly realized the lack of love within me, I found myself confessing to God: "I am sincerely sorry, God. I was not paying any attention to my mentees' needs. I had only wished them well through my words, not actions. I am so sorry. I now realize they are souls You have entrusted to me."

Tears filled my eyes again. I did not exactly understand what was happening to me, but one fact was made clear. One thing was for sure, I do not have enough love within me to pour into others. I realized that day that unless the Lord pours His love into me, I cannot love my mentees the way I wanted to love them.

> Suppose a brother or a sister is without clothes and daily food. If one of you says to them, "Go in peace; keep warm and well fed," but does nothing about their physical needs, what good is it?
>
> JAMES 2:15-16 NIV

I Had No Love to Give My Mentees

As I reflected on this verse, I felt ashamed for not being more sensitive to the needs of the people around me. I was disappointed in myself. So, I simultaneously prayed for God to pour His love into me.

If You Focus on Others' Successes, God Will Take Care of Yours

That day, my mentees witnessed my tears of shame. I told them, "I am sincerely sorry." It was an apology for not being able to meet their needs. Judging from my personality, this is something that does not usually happen in the relationship between a professor and a student, so it has become a special moment in my memory. It was also a situation that helped me realize that I can change my stubborn self when I am filled with the Holy Spirit.

That very weekend, in the early morning, I found time to set up an interview practice meeting. Due to the COVID-19 pandemic, in-person interviews were impossible. So, this became the perfect opportunity for me to help my mentees become more used to the new format of online interviews. Seeing my mentees all dressed up, nervously yet professionally addressing all my questions, I understood this was a great idea, and I was thankful to God. Through this practice, I also had the unexpected benefit of being able to understand the lives and the values held by all my mentees. After this, our lab started holding annual preparation meetings around the interview season.

Can I Pray for You?

God poured His love not only into the clinic but also into the lab. My new goal in life is to help the people around me to succeed. It is my goal for my patients to recover and feel joy, but it is also my goal for my mentees to become academically excellent researchers and patient-centered physicians. I believe God will take care of my own success when I focus on the success of others. I dream that this word will come alive in my life: "Give, and it will be given to you. A good measure, pressed down, shaken together and running over, will be poured into your lap. For with the measure you use, it will be measured to you" (Luke 6:38 NIV).

Strongly Believing That I Was Right

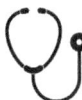

God's Love Pours into the Home

I once raised my voice when I was talking with my daughter at home. I shouted at her, "How could you be so rude to me?" We were both offended by each other. Then, suddenly, it seemed God was saying to me, "Do you think you are important? Is it that important how you are treated?"

I was taken aback. I had never once thought of the situation that way. I had always thought that I should discipline my children when they misbehave. At that moment, I realized I loved myself more than I loved my child. I had been angry because I strongly believed that I was not a person to be treated with disrespect. These thoughts brought tears to my eyes. "God," I prayed, "I'm sorry. I was wrong. I'm truly sorry."

Soon after, I asked my daughter for forgiveness. I must die, and Christ has to live in me. But it is truly difficult to reach this state. I can feel my ego, which I once thought was dead, jump back to life several times a day. Even when I talk to my wife and children at home, my "dead" ego keeps wriggling back to life. This is why I proclaim Galatians 2:20 every morning: "I have been crucified with Christ; and it is no longer I who live, but Christ lives in me; and the life which I now live in the flesh I live by faith in the Son of God, who loved me and gave Himself up for me" (NASB).

This was also the day when God poured out His love on me and, paradoxically, made me realize that I had none of my own love to give. He made me realize once again that His love can be poured into me and flow only when I realize there is no love in me.

In the past, I would become impatient when things did not go the direction I wanted; I tried to push what I believed was best onto others rather than humbly listening to their needs. Once, I went on a trip with a loved one. I was greatly prepared for the trip, investing both time and money in the journey. When my loved one suddenly fell ill and could not go on the trip, I felt more upset by the fact that we could not go on the trip than the fact that someone I loved was sick. Could there be better proof that there was no love in me?

Dad Will Do Better

I have come to realize that true love is more about worrying about the health of the person I love that worrying about my own feelings. In the past, I had believed it was better to be *less* concerned about the people around me; this was in

Strongly Believing That I Was Right

contrast to my wife, who constantly worried about others. I was arrogant in this regard. Once again, God helped me realize that I am truly a person without love—someone who does not care for anyone, someone who does not fully listen to and empathize with others. I recognized that the reason for my lack of worry was my lack of love. I was saddened by this, but also grateful for the revelation.

Now I seek love above all that can be sought. The words of 1 Corinthians resonate in my heart: "If I have the gift of prophecy and can fathom all mysteries and all knowledge, and if I have a faith that can move mountains, but do not have love, I am nothing. If I give all I possess to the poor and give over my body to hardship that I may boast, but do not have love, I gain nothing" (1 Corinthians 13:2–3 NIV). Now I know all too well that I am nothing unless His love is poured into my heart.

In a poem entitled "Resemblance," which I wrote while thinking of my children, I confess, "Dad will do better/Dad is becoming more like Jesus/It will get better//Imagine the day/when you/are proud/that you/are like Daddy//And the day/that Jesus will/rejoice/that you/are like Him."

Oblivious

by
Young Kwang Chae

When I said I did not know myself,
You said You know me.

When I said I did not know You,
You said You love me.

When I said I did not know the world,
You said You trust me.

When I said I did not know mercy,
You poured Your love on me.

When I said I did not know if I was capable,
You showed me Your work.

But now it is alright even if I don't know.
It is alright because I know You are with me.

Keyword 1

Friend: accompanying with a confession that I don't have love in me

In the book of Romans, the apostle Paul said this:

> Not only so, but we also glory in our sufferings, because we know that suffering produces perseverance; perseverance, character; and character, hope.
> —ROMANS 5:3–4 NIV

We become infinitely humble and poor in spirit through a series of trials that leads to tribulation, patience, and a refined character. I love the verse that follows: "And hope does not put us to shame, because God's love has been poured out into our hearts through the Holy Spirit, who has been given to us" (Romans 5:5 NIV). As seen from my previous stories, unless God fills my heart with His love every day through the Holy Spirit, there is no hope for me to be able to love others in the way I want to love them.

It seems the Holy Spirit pours out His love when we confess we are not ashamed of the hope found in Jesus. If anyone realizes that they don't have true love in themselves as I did, wouldn't it be impossible to love with arrogance?

Keyword 1 ....

Moreover, when you realize there is no love in you, you will not be ashamed of the hope of the life you have found in Jesus; you can free yourself from misunderstandings and persecutions. Even if I fall due to my lack of love, I know I will be renewed each day with His love.

Ever since I realized that I cannot live a single day without God's love, I pray every day to Him to fill my heart with His love. This is an earnest prayer to Him to salvage my life. But even in that moment, paradoxically, joy finds its way into my heart. It is much like Jeremiah's confession: "They [God's mercies] are new every morning, great is your faithfulness" (Lamentations 3:23 NIV). Every day, I am full of excitement and thanksgiving because I feel God's love pouring out when I pray, meet the Lord, or read His Word.

Jesus spoke these words to Simon Peter at the Last Supper: "But I have prayed for you, Simon, that your faith may not fail. And when you have turned back, strengthen your brothers" (Luke 22:32 NIV). As such, Jesus was always Someone who interceded for His disciples. However, when they were up on the Mount of Olives, before He died on the cross, He asked His disciples to pray for Him. "Then he said to them, 'My soul is overwhelmed with sorrow to the point of death. Stay here and keep watch with me'" (Matthew 26:38 NIV). He also prayed to the heavenly Father, "My Father, if it is possible, may this cup be taken from me. Yet not as I will, but as you will" (verse 39 NIV).

I often consider why Jesus, who had to endure not only physical pain but also emotional suffering, asked His

Keyword 1

disciples to pray with Him so that God's heart and love could be poured out onto Him.

Likewise, why don't *we* ask *our* friends to pray for God's love to be poured into our own poor, loveless hearts? When God pours His love on us, that is when we can truly bear our own cross and fulfill His mission. There will be no revival and no "becoming more like Jesus" until you realize your unclean heart and your sins that will persist without God's love and love toward your neighbors. Where true repentance takes place, God's love is poured out through the Holy Spirit. I am so grateful I was able to realize this and share this secret with you.

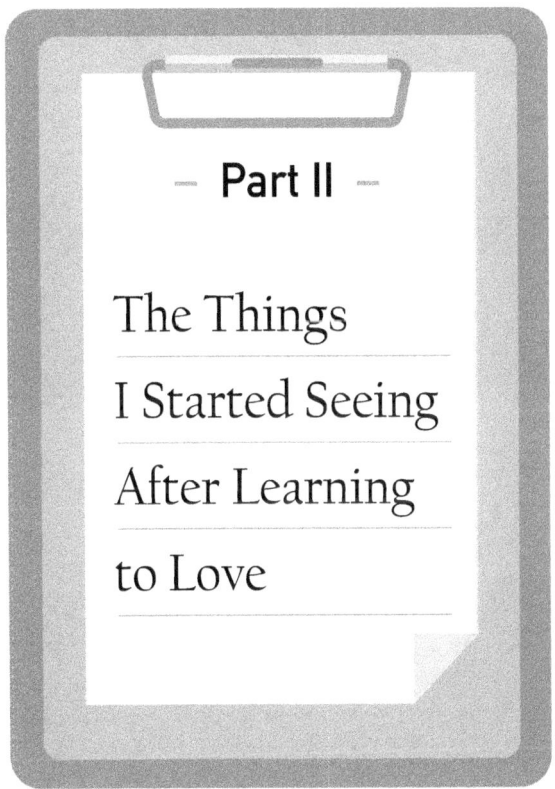

Part II

The Things I Started Seeing After Learning to Love

I Found Honor in My Name

The "glory" of my family is a literal phenomenon. Because my name is *Young Kwang*, which means "glory" in Korean, some people have asked me if I was born into a Christian family. My parents are believers now, but they weren't when I was born. My name was given to me in the hope that I would someday become the glory of the family.

When I was growing up, I was a quiet, but also positive and confident child. I grew up quite comfortably, thanks to my parents, who loved me dearly. As I enjoyed learning new things, I was a good student. I was also quite popular, and I had many friends; in high school, I was elected president of the student council. I also enjoyed studying logic; I remember enjoying preparing for the writing section that was introduced in my college entrance exam.

At that time, the *Hankook Ilbo* (a Korean daily newspaper company) held essay contests, and many students submitted their writing. The winning essays were published in the paper. Because many of my articles had appeared in the newspaper, most of my college friends had heard of me before we even met.

My writings were even used in essay-writing textbooks at that time. A professor of Korean literature studies at Seoul National University evaluated me positively, saying, "Mr. Chae's skills have been proven. He no longer needs to submit his writings." When I applied to medical school, I had the vague idea that I wanted to do something to directly help other people. But I was quite arrogant in that I did not want to go to any school other than the best university. I only applied to one medical school—Seoul National University Medical School—and I was accepted.

In college, I enjoyed going to school, learning new things, and making friends. Then I started attending church for an odd reason: I thought I could learn English by attending the new English services the local church was offering. I also enjoyed singing, so I immediately applied for the church choir once I heard they were recruiting. I also remember going to a place where foreign workers gathered during Christmas and performing with the choir in a Christmas cantata there.

I soon became curious about the Bible study groups that were offered to college students. My friends joined, so I did, as well. I was taken aback by the extremely friendly atmosphere of the community; people even celebrated my birthday, and they always welcomed me, after only having known each other a short amount of time.

Could I Also Become God's Glory?

As I was slowly learning about the church community, I decided to attend the college winter retreat they offered. A long bus ride took us into the countryside. Once we arrived at the retreat site, we laid cushions on the floor and sat in groups. Our instructor was an Indonesian missionary, and we listened intently to his message. As I listened to him, I began to believe that God had created the universe—and He had created me. I believed that He is my Father. The missionary's words permeated my heart as he explained that He who created and operated the whole world knows all about me and loves me. I was amazed that He even knew my name before the universe was created. Indeed, in Jeremiah 1:5, God said to Jeremiah, "Before I formed you in the womb I knew you" (NIV). And Paul wrote in Ephesians 1:4, "He chose us in Him [Christ] before the foundation of the world" (NKJV).

What also shocked me was that God apparently loved me so much that He had sent His only Son to carry a heavy cross, upon which He would die to atone for my sins. I almost could not believe these words because they were so amazing, but I also realized that all I had to do was to gratefully accept God's love.

So, I opened the door of my heart and invited Jesus in to become my Master. I confessed to God for the first time, "I love You, God." Strangely, in that moment, I experienced joy and a sense of peace I had never felt before.

Can I Pray for You?

The lyrics of a hymn I loved at that time began like this: "All that I am, all that I have, I lay them down before You, O Lord." It felt so good to know there was a God to whom I could give everything I had. I started weeping for no reason whenever I sang this hymn.

The hymn ends as follows: "Things in the past, things yet unseen, wishes and dreams that are yet to come true. All of my hopes, all of my plans, my heart and my hands are lifted to You." I was incredibly grateful for the fact that the Master of my life was no longer myself, but God.

However, despite this gratefulness, it took quite a while for my stubborn self to go through an actual change. I had other priorities. If I had an exam coming up on Monday, I wouldn't go to church on Sunday. I used to think that people who attend church on weekdays were either fanatics or people who really had nothing to do. I thought I should instead spend more time on my own self-improvement. I resented anyone trying to force me to do something other than what I wanted to do. I believed in moderation; I wanted to become a person who excelled both in the church and in the world.

There used to be a nightclub in the basement of the building where the college church community gatherings took place. After these gatherings, I would often hang out with my friends in that nightclub. I wanted to become a "cool" person both in the church and in the world, so I worked hard in multiple settings simultaneously: the church college community, my classical guitar club, and the hip-hop dance club.

I slowly began to change without realizing it. The constant prayers and encouragement of my current wife, whom I was dating at the time, played a very critical role in this change. My wife later told me that she prayed for me to grow closer to God and to love the church community. God answered her prayers. Once I graduated from medical school and started working as a public health doctor, I came to truly love the youth community to which I had belonged at that church. As someone who used to fall asleep as soon as the sermon started, I had changed so much. I am always thankful to my wife because I owe her so much for the Gospel.

I enjoyed worshiping God with the members of the youth community. With them, I discovered the joy of praying together to ask for God's guidance and provision in our lives and sharing stories of how He answered our prayers. We drew closer to God by sharing our lives and sincerely praying for each other. We started out as strangers and ended up becoming each other's soul mates.

To a Life Without Envy

Upon graduating from medical school, I immediately applied to the Korean military because I wanted to receive medical training in the United States. For three years, I worked as a public health doctor on the island of Daebudo, located on the west coast of Korea. In my last year as a public health doctor, I took my prayer request to God and attended morning prayer every single day for one full year. After praying for a long time, I made this confession to God for the first time: "God, regardless of whether You answer my prayers, I will always be content because I will always be Your child. You know what is best for me. I give my life to You, God. I want to know You and love You more."

I was amazed at myself for declaring my love for God in this way. After this confession, God began to answer my prayers as if He had been waiting for this exact moment. Looking back on this prayer, I am now convinced that I have come so far in my life because I surrendered my life to the Lord.

When I was in my fourth year of medical school, I decided to study abroad in the United States. I wanted to study medicine on a bigger stage. One thought, however, held me back: I was afraid of falling behind my peers. I imagined what it would be like ten or twenty years in the future: I would be treating cancer patients at an academic medical center while my friends in Korea would have already opened their private clinics and be more financially well off than me.

I was in a phase where I valued material success over anything else. However, I was well aware that I could not be happy if I kept comparing myself to others. I remembered my seniors telling me, "One of my classmates from medical school used to struggle in academics, and now he earns more than I do. He's the most successful one in our class. I don't understand why I didn't choose a specialty that earns more." Although I could not be any more specific, I was determined to "succeed" in this world.

I Found Honor in My Name

But did I *really* need worldly success in life? I knew that I should separate the idea of "living well" from success or wealth. Even if you are poor, you can live well and be successful. Even if you are rich, you may live in extreme anxiety and depression, thinking about suicide every day. Language is a system of thought. When we use language to describe the rich and those living comfortably, we confine our minds within a worldly frame. The world judges success by a person's job salary. Following this logic, comparing myself to others is easy because salaries are quantitative.

I asked my fellow Christian friend to pray for me, that I would stop comparing myself to others and live my life for the Lord with gratitude and joy. I also sought help from my pastors. I prayed earnestly that I would not envy anything but the knowledge of God. A few years later, when I was studying in Baltimore, Maryland, I was invited to a mansion that looked like a castle to me. To my surprise, I felt grateful to God. My old self would have responded with either a sigh, frustrated at my own salary and my belongings, or an ambitious promise to myself that I would work harder and eventually make enough money to afford such a place. That day, however, I felt confident, believing that living in a fancy house would not mean anything if I did not fear Jesus Christ. God might even bless me one day with a house like that. A song began to play in my head: "What matters where on earth we dwell? On a mountaintop or in a dell, in a cottage or a mansion fair, where Jesus is, 'tis heaven there." God had answered our prayers: I had finally broken my habit. I was completely satisfied in the Lord alone. I was overwhelmed with gratitude.

When I become spiritually dull, Satan will sneak up to me and ask, "What have you been doing while your peers are basking in their success? Why do you have to struggle so much? Don't you think you're wasting your life?" Then my answer will be, "The Lord is my shepherd; I shall not want" (Psalm 23:1 KJV).

The Joy of Walking with Him

During my three years as a public health doctor, I passed all three portions of the U.S. Medical Licensing Examination (USMLE). For the last phase, I had to travel to Hawaii, the closest testing site, given that the test was not offered in Korea. This was an exam in which one would have to sit in front of a computer and answer questions for eight hours a day for two days. I took the exam alone, having studied the day before at a hotel on the Waikiki beachfront.

With the simple thought that I didn't want to waste the money I'd spent on plane tickets, I planned a day for sightseeing. I sunbathed alone on the Waikiki beach and went snorkeling in Hanauma Bay. However, it did not feel right. The weather was wonderful, the scenery was beautiful, and the environment was perfect for snorkeling, but I wasn't very happy. There was no one around for me to share the good things I was experiencing. I was wandering around alone in a place where family and lovers come to have fun, and suddenly I was struck with loneliness.

Then I realized something: What matters more than where you go is who you are going with. No matter how barren a place may be, if I am with my beloved wife and children, I would want to live on that land. Likewise, if I walk with my Lord Jesus, it does not matter what my circumstances are.

God wants to give us the joy of walking with Him. It is the heart of God the Father that He always wants to be with us, His children. Like the lyrics of the hymn, I realized that if I really "walk with the Lord Jesus," "the kingdom of heaven is everywhere." When I give my appearance, my possessions, all my hopes, and all my plans to the Lord, they are no longer mine, but the Lord's. I fully believe that He will take full responsibility for them when I decide to walk beside Him.

After Meeting You

by
Young Kwang Chae

Please keep it a secret
That I was a sociopath.

Please keep it a secret
That I was a selfish villain.
Life was a survival game,
And the world was a talent show.

Why this child is crying
And that child is angry with me
Was a puzzle to me.

But I
I met You as if it were fate,
Became a new person.

Your tears still flow through my soul,
The path of water that burst.
Remembering the sky-colored sea,
Gathering the tears of neighbors,
It became a river.

Thank You.
After meeting You,
I found more reasons to cry.
After meeting You,
I began to love others.

Becoming a Novice Coordinator

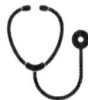

I Can Help

After I finished my service in the Korean military, I left to study in the United States while most of my friends stayed at Seoul National University Hospital to complete their residency. It was daunting to head to the States alone. However, my desire to learn new things in a new environment trumped my fears. Thankfully, I was offered a scholarship from Samsung during my last year as a public health doctor.

I immediately began pursuing my double master's degree in public health and business administration at Johns Hopkins University. I majored in medical statistics. During this process, I made many long-lasting friendships. At that time, our school's motto was "Saving a Million Lives at a Time." Starting from my second year, I was given the opportunity to work as a postdoc researcher in the cancer research laboratory at Johns Hopkins Medical School, concurrently with my studies. During this period, I was able to broaden my horizons in medical research. I enjoyed learning basic medical research to study the mechanisms of cancer development and clinical medical research through the blood and cancer tissue samples provided by patients undergoing cancer treatment. It seems that the foundation for the translational research I am doing currently, which is a bridge from the bench side to the bedside, was laid at this time.

The master's program I had entered started in July, while the other courses usually started in September. The first month, I became acquainted with the Johns Hopkins Public Health Christian Fellowship. Every Wednesday around lunchtime, we gathered in the school meeting room to have a meal together, study the Bible, and share what was going on in our lives. Shortly after the summer quarter, I received an email from the group's executive team about finding someone to help organize this fellowship. So, I promptly sent a reply saying, "I can help."

To my surprise, I later learned that I was the only one who replied to that email. Everyone from the executive team was graduating, so they were all leaving Baltimore before September. So, starting from the autumn semester, I became the president of the group and served all the students. Before that moment, I had never thought I would be able to serve as a president of a community. I didn't think I was capable enough of leading a group, but I was available to share my time and my heart. It felt like an amazing coincidence that I had begun to spread the Gospel and experience the blessings of sharing the Gospel with my church youth community, where students from all over the world gathered in one place. God had been preparing me all along for this position.

If I Make Myself Available, God Will Work through Me

I came across an organization called the Korean Students Abroad (KOSTA), an annual conference held in Chicagoland for Christian students and professionals from all over the United States. It was a gathering where Christian students and professionals came together in the first week of July each year to listen to the Word and share their lives. My wife, children, and I attended the retreat almost every year, and the grace we received was truly significant.

During my first KOSTA experience, there was a TM (task major) KOSTA meeting in which people of the same major gathered to discuss and present their academic concerns from a Christian perspective. I applied to the biology major group while serving on the preparation team. It bothered me that there was no representation from the "medical" field. At that time, after reading the book *The Foolish Doctor*, I was deeply moved by the idea of living as a Christian physician. I prayed to God, asking for guidance on how to proceed. In my heart, I wanted to invite the late Dr. Ahn Soo-hyun, the author of that book, to the meeting. During my prayer, I felt God's message: Would you serve in his place?

I sensed God's desire to share the spirit and missional life of the late Dr. Ahn Soo-hyun with the attendees. I contacted the KOSTA organizers and shared my intention. As there were no other volunteers from the medical field, I have been serving in medical seminars since my first year at KOSTA until now.

The blessings my attendees and I received through the medical seminar far exceeded my expectations. The seminar became a place for many aspiring medical students and current medical professionals to gain strength in the Lord. One international student who was battling pancreatic cancer requested prayer, and I prayed with tears for him. Some even told me that prayer requests they brought with them to the retreat were answered after the seminar. Through these experiences, I have come to realize that when I rely on and obey God, who is greater than my abilities, He works. Furthermore, I've learned that in places where few are willing to volunteer, without fierce competition, the likelihood of God's calling is higher. I finally understood the process by which I became the president of the Johns Hopkins Public Health Christian Fellowship and the coordinator of the KOSTA medical seminar—I was given these positions without even really trying or having to compete with others, because God wanted me to serve in these places. One of the "Ten Commandments of Career Choice" given at Geochang High School, a mission school in Korea, is to "Avoid where everything is set up, and choose a wasteland where you have to start from scratch. Never go to a place where people are vying for each other. Go where no one goes." Perhaps it's in places like these that we can experience God's astonishing work through us and receive the unexpected gift of deeper trust in Him.

Keyword 2

Direction: learning from the heart of the vineyard owner

The parable of the workers in the vineyard in Matthew 20 begins like this:

> "For the kingdom of heaven is like a landowner who went out early in the morning to hire workers for his vineyard."
> —MATTHEW 20:1 NIV

It is difficult to understand the metaphor that heaven is like a vineyard owner. In this parable, a vineyard owner goes out to the street to look for workers and brings them back to the vineyard. Workers then start their work at different times: one at six in the morning, and others at nine, noon, and three o'clock. Some workers even arrive at five in the afternoon, when there is far less work to do than there was in the morning. Nonetheless, the owner pays them equally for the day's work.

When I first read this parable, I thought, *Where is the fairness in this? Isn't receiving rewards based on one's effort a reasonable idea?* For a long time, I could not accept this parable. It was uncomfortable to think that such a place could

Keyword 2 ....

be considered "heaven." Denying fair compensation to the workers felt contradictory to the spirit of capitalism, and I empathized with the workers' sense of injustice for receiving the same wage despite differing efforts, just as I felt unjust.

But one day, I realized before God that I, too, was a sinner without any qualifications. Only then did I understand that even the worker who worked all day couldn't have received the wage—or even the opportunity to work without the owner's grace. Everything is based on grace; but I, who lacked insight, had quickly turned grace into dissatisfaction by comparing between workers.

I never considered the thought that I might be the one who worked for only one hour at the end of the day. I was spiritually arrogant.

In fact, at that moment, my heart was similar to the heart of the older brother in the parable of the prodigal son found in Luke 15. The younger son left home after taking his share of his father's inheritance, wasted it all, and returned in rags. The father embraced and celebrated the prodigal son. However, the older son was displeased with this celebration, as he didn't understand his father's heart. He lacked gratitude because he didn't have the love of his father in his heart. He valued himself above all else, making him susceptible to the trap of comparison. I still periodically examine whether the heart of the older brother has seeped into my heart.

And so, I try to understand the heart of the vineyard owner, which is God's heart. The vineyard in the parable

Keyword 2

is not a place to make a profit by commercializing grapes. Rather, it is a place to give wages to laborers. From a worldly perspective, the workers may seem to be merely producing grapes, but from God's perspective, they are precious children to be embraced and loved. In other words, the vineyard is where God the Father gathers His children, feeding and clothing them.

Likewise, our workplaces are also the heavenly Father's vineyard. We should understand the owner's heart and serve others with this understanding. Serving people with this heart at home, school, work, or anywhere else is undoubtedly what God desires and delights in the most. Our heavenly Father's love is a love the world can hardly comprehend.

A Surprise Gift from Morning Prayers

I Called You and Your Family as One

My first year at Johns Hopkins University was devoted to studying public health and health service management. From the second year onward, I conducted cancer research simultaneously in the Johns Hopkins Medical School laboratory. I came to understand how impactful research can change the world, and I learned how to conduct methodologically sound studies. In the lab, I cultured cells and designed experiments to test hypotheses, discovering how fascinating research could be.

Of course, life in the laboratory was lonely and challenging. When experiments didn't progress as expected, feelings of frustration arose. It was especially difficult when I felt like I didn't have the mentorship I desired. During this time, my first daughter, Lina, was born. The delayed financial support that had been promised from the lab made the struggles of our whole family even greater.

A Surprise Gift from Morning Prayers

Amidst these circumstances, in my third year of study, I received an unexpected notice from the laboratory manager. At that time, I had completed the master's program on a student visa (F visa), and I was working in the lab under the Optional Practical Training (OPT) visa, which allowed me to work for one year after graduation while seeking employment. However, due to a change in school policy, I was informed that I could no longer remain in the lab; I was told to pack up and leave immediately. I was dumbfounded. I quickly froze all the cells I had been working with and packed away all my experiment notes into boxes. I was so shocked and taken aback that I didn't even have the space in my heart to feel sad. The period during which I had suddenly lost my place to work was a considerable amount of time until I started the premedical process at a U.S. hospital. It was a rough and chaotic time.

Up until that time, I had been awarded proportionally to the amount of effort I put into work. Recognition followed as much as I studied or displayed leadership. However, when God humbled me, there was nothing I could do through my own efforts. The days when snow endlessly fell and obscured my vision, making driving difficult—even the day I had to drive all the way from Baltimore to the snow-covered Canadian border because I needed to change my visa to a tourist visa to stay in the United States—I crossed the U.S. border at Niagara Falls, but I didn't have the leisure to appreciate its beauty. I struggled significantly during the times when I was out of work and had to stay home. I was jealous of people who had jobs. The worst times were when I had to consolidate my projects into a thesis. I was yearning for work, even if that meant I could not see patients as a doctor. God was breaking my arrogance and the misconception that I could achieve my success on my own.

I knew another physician who was working at a different research center and preparing for his surgical residency. We carpooled early every morning to attend church, which was over thirty minutes away by highway. We both cried out to God. We sought Him every day in the wilderness.

When I asked God why He had me go through this difficult time, He answered, "I am calling you and your family to come together and unite as one." It suddenly occurred to me that I had been thinking of myself as the main character of my life and my family as the supporting characters. I finally understood that God wanted me to work with my family as one team.

I then thought about my life. My wife had left her job to come to the United States with me. She was raising our child alone in a foreign land without any family nearby to help her. In addition, she was feeling stressed about her upcoming Uniform Certified Public Accountant (CPA) Examination. While I was out of work, God allowed me to take the time to focus on my wife and my family.

According to Acts 16:31, God's salvation is not given to me alone, but it is offered to me and my family as one bundle. Strangely enough, I could bear the pain more easily once I

A Surprise Gift from Morning Prayers

came to know the heart of our Father. Knowing the reason for the hardships allowed me to anticipate the God who would work through this process. Even when hospital life is tough now, when I think back to those days, all complaints vanish, and gratitude emerges naturally. I even wonder how it would have been if I hadn't gone through those times of difficulty. Perhaps I would have become an overly proud person who greatly undervalued my current life. Through this, I came to understand there is no wasted time in a life with God.

The Life-Saving Power of Household Chores

Toward the end of my days in the wilderness, I received a surprise gift from God. By God's grace, I was accepted to my top-choice residency program: the Einstein Medical Center in eastern Philadelphia. The Einstein Medical Center was one of the few hospitals at that time to offer permanent employment in the United States to medical residents. Unfortunately, the center no longer offered this benefit the year I entered. However, based on the papers I had written during my time at the Johns Hopkins research lab, I learned I could apply for a visa on an individual basis, and thankfully, our family's visa was approved just two months after applying. Throughout my residency, I was always grateful to have a workplace and patients to care for. I also mentored junior residents, for which I received the Best Resident Award.

During my final year at Einstein Medical Center, I was accepted to my top choice: the Hematology & Oncology fellowship program at the MD Anderson Cancer Center in Houston, Texas. God had led me through the wilderness in Baltimore, and now He had prepared unexpected gifts for me in Philadelphia.

During my time in Baltimore, I realized how important my time spent at home was. Household chores were repetitive and mundane, but I came to understand that these tasks truly contribute to making a home a home and taking care of family members. Mission work begins at home; the work at home is just as precious as the work in any other remote area of the world. That's why I refer to all mothers and fathers who nurture their homes as "home ministers," "home missionaries."

Everything Led Up to This Moment

On-Call Duty with the Lord

When I was working as an internal medicine doctor in Philadelphia during an on-call shift, I received a call from the emergency room to attend to two patients who had just arrived. Coincidentally, both patients had the last name of "Kim," and they were Korean-speaking individuals struggling with the English language. I hurried down to the ER and conducted consultations with them in Korean, prescribed medications, and completed their admission procedures.

At that moment, a thought struck me: *"God truly loves these people. He allowed me to take the USMLE, called me to Philadelphia, and used me to take care of them in my mother tongue. While I had been pursuing my own aspirations of becoming a doctor, could it be that God's purpose in using me wasn't for what I was aiming for?* This train of thought simplified things for me. And this confession emerged within me: "Thank You so much, Lord. I have only one desire. Even if

Can I Pray for You?

my life is full of achievements, if I am not used by You, my life is nothing. My only desire is to be used by You, Lord."

I recall a Korean grandmother. She wasn't my patient, but a nurse asked me to pass on a message from her. Her husband had gone into the operating room, and she was alone, feeling lost in an empty hospital room. I wanted to offer some words of comfort, but she was so anxious that the words "Can I pray for you?" unexpectedly came out of my mouth. She replied, "Thank you." Holding her hands tightly, I prayed. As soon as I opened the prayer with "Our God," I choked up. His love was too strong. I had to pause for a moment or two to calm my emotions. I was so embarrassed to see myself crying in front of someone I had just met, but she also cried with me. During the prayer, a confession emerged: "How much our God must love you, Grandma, to have stopped me, a passerby, and led me to pray for you!" I earnestly asked Him to pour out His love, comfort, and peace into her. I prayed for her husband, whom I had never met, for his healing and recovery. To me, prayer is the key that allows us to experience God's presence anytime, anywhere.

In Esther 4:14 (NIV), Mordecai spoke to his cousin, Queen Esther, whom he had raised like his own daughter: "Who knows whether it is not for this time that you have obtained the status of a queen?" Esther responded in verse 16, "And if I perish, I perish." This story resonated with me. Living in a specific neighborhood in the United States, studying at a particular school, and working at a specific job could all have been part of God's planned encounters for a purpose. Amid all the processes of achieving what I wanted, witnessing how God orchestrates His own way and brings forth good out of cooperation in the midst of fulfilling His purpose was truly amazing. As I realized that the reason God had placed me here in the United States might be for "such a time," my daily routine transformed into a prayer, and I desired that each day would become the very "time" God had prepared.

Where Did the Courage Come From?

On another day of duty, there was an elderly white grandfather who was admitted as a terminal lung cancer patient. The man, who was skin and bones, complained of bloody sputum and shortness of breath. After treating his pneumonia and stabilizing his overall condition, I went back to the on-call room. Strangely, I kept thinking of that elderly man. So, despite feeling tired and desiring rest, I frequently visited his room to be a companion to him.

At one point in our conversation, I said, "Humans are spiritual beings, don't you think?" After taking a few minutes to gather his thoughts, he responded that he thought the same way and had read many Buddhist books. I asked, "Have you ever been to a Christian church service before?" He said he hadn't. I don't know where the courage came from, but I boldly told the elderly man, "I go to church, and I believe in eternal life after death. It is a gift you receive when you believe in Jesus."

He was curious and wanted to know more about my faith. Slowly, I explained the Gospel I had learned from the Bible. Then, he asked how he could receive the gift of eternal life. So, I replied: "You can follow me in prayer in order to accept God into your heart."

As I began the prayer of acceptance, surprisingly the grandfather followed along, repeating each sentence after me. Eventually, that early morning, he accepted the Lord as his Savior. Overjoyed, I told him, "Heaven is having a feast to celebrate this day!"

I could feel the Lord's heart rejoicing over the man's salvation. It was truly a fulfilling moment. Actually, I could have taken a brief nap in the on-call room due to my exhaustion. However, when I obediently shared God's message in such a simple way, the Lord took over. The response to my prayer, in which I had asked God to use me for "such a time," had become my everyday reality.

The End of the Earth Is under My Feet

The Prayer Group That Saved Me

During my residency training in Philadelphia, I had a vague desire to share about God with my colleagues and join in intercessory prayer for patients. I prayed to God, asking if He could allow a prayer group to form within the hospital. However, prayer itself felt challenging due to the demanding nature of my medical training, and it seemed nearly impossible to gather everyone with their different schedules. Yet, I prayed with the thought, *Lord, this is Your work, so please make it happen.* Ultimately, God Himself orchestrated the formation of the prayer group.

Around that time, I had been serving as a medical seminar coordinator for KOSTA, which was held in Chicago every year. One time, I was asked to speak at a Youth KOSTA event (a Christian gathering for Korean American youth) focused on the "Missional Life." I still don't know why they chose me, not a pastor, to be the speaker on this topic. I had no prior experience in youth ministry, and I had never been on a mission trip before, so I was puzzled why I was asked to speak on "Missional Life" at a youth conference. However, as I prepared my speech, I had a small desire that the youth would experience the same God who worked in my life through my words.

The conference coincided with Thanksgiving, and I was on duty in the hospital during that time. I thought that no one could cover my duty for me. However, when I started to pray, telling the Lord that I would do it if it was His will, astonishingly, a colleague offered to cover my duty. It was a miracle, a work of God. Thanks to this, I could offer the "Missional Life" seminar to the youth and plant seeds of God's dreams in them.

Upon arriving at the event venue, I discovered that the instructors were using their spare time to consult with the students. Surprisingly, many young people aspiring to become medical professionals approached me for counseling. Among them were those who were facing difficulties in applying to medical schools or hospitals due to their lack of U.S. permanent residency, similar to the challenges I had faced when applying to U.S. hospitals with no permanent residency. As I listened to their stories and shared my own experiences, I could realize why God had brought me from my role as a medical resident at the Pennsylvania hospital to serve at the Youth KOSTA retreat in Maryland.

Following the retreat, I shared this story with a pastor I knew. He then asked me to share my testimony with the youth group at his church in New Jersey. I willingly passed along the same message to this group, this time in English. Afterward, the church sent me a recorded file of my testimony. While I had always wanted to share the Gospel with my colleagues at the hospital, it was challenging to find the time and place to do so on an individual basis. That's why I had the idea to give my colleagues a CD with a recording of my testimony. Even though I felt shy about it, I thought it might be a good way to share my story: "It's the story of my life. I hope you enjoy it."

Once, I was having a Quiet Time (QT) in the hospital library, when Athan, a second-year resident from Greece, walked up to me and asked me what I was doing. Starting with the definition of *QT*, I naturally started talking about my belief in God. Eventually, I gave him the CD with my testimony that I happened to have with me. Of course, I handed it over with some hesitation, wondering if he would even listen to it. However, the next day, I could not believe my ears when he said, "I think I need a prayer meeting." The Lord must have opened up his heart.

I had given him the CD simply with the intention of introducing him to the Jesus I knew, but the Lord went beyond my imagination and stirred his heart to ask if we could pray together. Through his words, I felt the voice of God urging me to pray with him. As a result, a prayer group started. And then, God continued to send people to the group. I cannot forget the time when I had conversations and prayed with Athan about the essence of the Gospel and the act of surrendering our lives to Jesus. After receiving the Lord that day, Athan said things I had only seen in books: "The world looks different now; the trees outside the hospital are so beautiful. My whole life has changed." It was amazing how my small act of obedience in the Youth KOSTA ministry had led to the salvation of Athan's soul.

As Athan's faith grew astonishingly, he transformed into an encouraging fellow worker who uplifted me. Whenever I was going through tough times, he was the first one I asked for prayer. Back when I had started working in Houston, I was once in trouble because my on-call schedule suddenly changed; a fellow resident had failed to keep his promise. When I called Athan, he said, before he even heard the details, "Don't worry. I will cover for you." He was on his busiest rotation, and he was on call only two days ago. Knowing his situation, I burst into tears of thankfulness. As a result, I had the chance to attend a specialized cardiology course I had been wanting to attend. He also suggested that we should forgive my co-worker, who hadn't kept his promise, and instead pray together in love. As Jesus declares in the gospel of Matthew, "The first will be last and the last first" (NET).

Athan received a special gift from God. During a two-week vacation period, he was assigned a "duty day." Even though he believed it was an unjust situation that could easily be fixed, he chose to take the duty during his vacation time for the sake of his other colleagues, rather than protesting. He thought that maybe all of this could be God's will. As a result, that day, he unexpectedly encountered a fellow senior staff member with whom he had worked in the cardiology department. Through this unplanned meeting, Athan landed his dream job as a cardiology fellow.

I have often witnessed God working through Athan. Later, when my mentee ran into him by chance at a hospital in Pennsylvania, my mentee recognized him immediately, took a photo with him, and sent it to me. It felt like "God's comfort," summoning beautiful memories.

From Work to the Mission Field

Upon completing my residency and during my fellowship in oncology at MD Anderson Cancer Center, I often tuned in to internet Christian broadcasts in the duty room. Once, while watching an online Japanese culture event called *Love Sonata*, I fervently prayed for Japan. Coincidentally, the very next day, a Japanese medical student joined our bone-marrow transplant team. I shared many stories with that student over lunch. I told the student that I was grateful to the Japanese. I owed much of my faith to my wife, and her faith had been greatly influenced by my mother-in-law, who came to know God deeply through her Japanese friend in the United States. Before realizing it, I started telling the student, who didn't know God yet, about God's grace in my life.

The student listened attentively and expressed his intention to watch the online *Love Sonata* video—from his hometown of Yokohama—and think about his faith. It was such a coincidence for a Japanese student to show up the day after I had prayed for Japan. Witnessing this unexpected turn of events, I realized that God's hand was at work, directing the course of events beyond my imagination.

During my leukemia-related research at MD Anderson, I worked with a Vietnamese doctor. A desire arose in me to see him come to know God, and I started praying for him. Though he had spent a long time in research in the United States and was about to embark on a fellowship, his journey had not been without challenges. Gratefully, he and his family started attending a local church. I listened to him as he prayed before our meal together, "Jesus, please be the Lord of my life." I can't tell you how much I rejoiced over his spiritual birthday. I felt deep in my heart that, among the many reasons God had sent me all the way to Houston, one primary reason was the Lord's boundless love for this man's soul. I was truly happy that I was used as a channel of God's love. Although I had never been to Vietnam, I kept him, his family, and the nation of Vietnam in my prayers.

I also recall a moment of unexpected joy while working with patients in the hospital. I used to serve as the primary care physician for cancer patients in an underprivileged area outside Houston. One colorectal cancer patient I met at that time gave me a wonderful testimony every time we met. I would hold his hands, and we would pray together for comfort and strength. We even encouraged each other's faith through phone calls. Although this patient had terminal cancer, we believed the Lord had not given him more than he could handle. He testified that his own suffering had made God's compassion for people around him even greater. Whenever he had time, he would tell other patients about God and pray for them. Once, during my rounds, I remembered a story he had once told me, and tears streamed down my cheeks. It was truly a joy to get to know him in the hospital.

Through these moments, I naturally gravitated toward thinking about the missional life. I came to realize that the missional life can be lived anywhere at any time as long as I depend on and obey God. I could sense that God had called me to become a missionary, as He wanted to embrace the souls around me, in my campus, and in my workplace. My identity as a missionary became clear to me. While my life had previously revolved around my wants and needs, now my life was being guided by Jesus.

The reason God had led me to a specific area, a specific laboratory, and a specific hospital was to proclaim the Kingdom of God in those places. Although I could neither plan nor imagine my future, God had given me strength, passion, people, and opportunities for His mission. I held on to the belief that He would continue to plan out my future. Every morning, I would pray the following for other health-care workers, patients, and their families: "May God's Kingdom come and may salvation take place. Lord, use me for Your work."

My identity as a "medical missionary" solidified when I felt God's heart breaking for His children. After attending the Youth KOSTA retreat, I was in tears every time I saw a patient. More often than not, I could physically feel his or her pain in my body; I remember when my white coat was drenched in tears, as I held hands and prayed with a middle-aged leukemia patient who needed hospitalization. The focus of my studies had been steadily shifting away from my own success and toward the care of my patients; praying for the leukemia patient made the most definite shift.

In Acts 1:8, Jesus says, "But you will receive power when the Holy Spirit comes on you; and you will be my witnesses in Jerusalem, and in all Judea and Samaria, and to the ends of the earth" (NIV). If Jerusalem is our "family," and Judea is our "relatives and friends," then Samaria is an enemy who was once a part of us. Where is "the ends of the earth"? It literally means the ends of the earth, a place that has nothing to do with me, a place I will die not knowing for the rest of my life if I do not go.

In my life, I met people who would otherwise have nothing to do with me for the rest of my life if I had not gone to the places where I went. The medically vulnerable patients I met in the emergency room in Philadelphia, where firearm injuries were frequent, were my "ends of the earth"; I would have had little chance of meeting them if I had not been working at that hospital.

My workplace became my "ends of the earth." When I go around the earth in a full circle, I return to the land on which I am standing. This, right here, is my "ends of the earth." In particular, the United States is a place where people from all over the world live together; I was grateful that God had called me as a "missionary" to my workplace in the United States, my "ends of the earth."

Words I Want to Hear from God

Picture Yourself Ten Years from Now

After completing my internal medicine training by His grace in Philadelphia, my family moved to Houston, Texas, where our second and third children were given to us as gifts from God. Unlike the East Coast, which has four distinct seasons, Houston is hot all year round, and since our children could always enjoy the outdoor swimming pool, they quickly fell in love with the area.

The MD Anderson Cancer Center, where I worked as a fellow, is one of America's most prestigious medical centers known for its frontline cancer research. Patients from all over the world arrive at MD Anderson expecting to receive the latest cancer treatments. I appreciated learning about many things, such as the development of new targeted therapies, research on biomarkers that determine cancer treatment methods and prognosis, and various targeted treatment clinical trials. I especially enjoyed combining various targeted therapies in creative ways and watching patients get better.

As I had done back in Philadelphia, I prayed that God would help me have prayer meetings with colleagues in this hospital. God answered my prayer through Chris, a fellow resident. Although he did not even know I was a Christian, he asked me during grand rounds, "Would you like to have a prayer meeting with me?" My answer was an obvious *yes*. While I did not have the courage to start one myself, God accomplished this task through the lips of another colleague.

God sent me another friend here named Hans. Every week before grand rounds, we would pray for our patients and colleagues and share our lives together. I had the privilege of leading him through the prayer of salvation.

When I was in high school, I thought that everyone in medical school would end up living the same life as doctors and specialists. Life, I later learned, was made up of a series of choices. When I was a resident, I thought that life after a hematology and oncology fellowship would be the same for everyone entering this path; it turned out that life can be very different, depending on whether one opens a business, stays in a university hospital, or specializes in a specific field. I decided to work in a university hospital as an oncologist with a subspecialty, because I wanted to combine clinic work, research, and education. However, it was difficult to choose which specific field to pursue; every field had its own charm.

Words I Want to Hear from God

I wanted to ask God for His opinion. I invited two friends to join me in morning prayers so that we could start the day together, share prayer requests, and pray for one another. We continued this ritual for forty days. It felt very special to me. Fortunately, I received His answer on the fortieth day. After rounding with a professor that afternoon, he called me into his lab to give me career advice. He asked me a couple of questions, then told me to close my eyes and imagine what I would be doing ten years from that time. I began to picture myself taking care of cancer patients and conducting clinical trials to develop new targeted therapies for my patients. When I told him about this vision, the professor suggested that the early therapeutics clinical trial subdivision would be a good fit for me. I could feel my tears as I walked out of the professor's lab. God had answered my prayers specifically.

Soon afterward, I became a codirector of the Early Clinical Trial Cancer Center at Northwestern University Hospital in Chicago. I also started serving as a vice chair of the largest clinical trial group in the United States, called the Early Therapeutics & Rare Cancer Committee of the Southwest Oncology Group (SWOG), where I plan and manage national clinical trials. God offered guidance to me and my colleagues when we were uncertain about our future.

You Are So Much Like Me

Although I had to make frequent moves, I was blessed to receive a warm welcome from every church I had attended.

Baltimore's small group for young couples, for example, gave my wife a beautiful baby shower; we still remember it to this day. I realized this was how it was to be loved within a community. I also learned the joy of sharing lives through our weekly morning QT. In Philadelphia, my wife and I started a book club with another married couple, and we have seen each other grow over time.

In Houston, a family that hosted our small group every week taught me how to "serve your own family." I also looked up to the professors from MD Anderson Cancer Center in our small group as I witnessed them serving their patients' families and visiting professors' families with love. When the visiting professors returned to Korea, they received blessings by knowing Jesus as their Lord and Savior. I was especially impressed by Professor Kim, approaching his retirement, who brought rice and his rice cooker all the way to a dormitory where a fourth-year international medical student had planned to stay for a month.

I lived in Baltimore, Philadelphia, and Houston, but I visited Chicago every summer to attend a KOSTA retreat. During the retreat, we would eat every meal together and pray for each other's families. Even though we were meeting for the first time, we learned that sharing the Gospel and praying for one another can be healing and uniting. I now realize the time I had spent before coming to Chicago trained me not only as a doctor, but also as a Christian; it taught me that small group sharing can be life-changing.

Words I Want to Hear from God

I enjoy listening to a famous pop song called "Still Fighting It"; the song was used as an original soundtrack in the drama *Itaewon Class*. It is about a father who goes through difficulties in life and tells his son that things are not going to be easy. This is what the lyrics say: "You're so much like me. I'm sorry." I can feel both his fatherly love and his sadness from wanting to do more for his son but being unable to do so. In contrast, our Father God, who can do anything, has made me His child. Out of love, Jesus carried the cross for me. God will be most pleased with me when I become more like Jesus. I often imagine Jesus telling me: "You are so much like Me. Thank you."

I remember a pastor who used to come to my church in Houston. He once said, "Our small group leaders are like pastors." He was moved by the way they served and loved small groups like their own families. From then on, whenever I prayed and listened to God's voice, I wanted to hear Him say, "You are so much like Me."

Keyword 3

Scar: My scars are my talents

People say that having a great mentor is the key to success. One of the things I looked forward to when I moved to the United States was finding the perfect mentor, learning from that person, and growing from their support. But unfortunately for me, the people whom I considered mentors disappeared one day—three times in a row. They were the ones who supported me in hardship and in trials at every turning point in my life and believed in me, but due to personal matters, they all had to step down from their positions as professors at university hospitals. Among them was a professor with whom I worked at the University of Texas MD Anderson Cancer Center; we lost contact the day before we were scheduled to meet at a conference in Chicago for a research meeting. I later found out that he had been sentenced to ten years in prison for attempted murder. These were the people who had said they would mentor me!

I lost my mentors three times in a row; it almost felt like I was in a movie. Although each loss left a scar on me, as I had been yearning for good mentoring, they also inspired me to become a good mentor for aspiring physicians.

Keyword 3

As I was completing my fellowship training in Houston, Professor Waun Ki Hong told me: "You don't need to find a mentor. You can be a mentor yourself." He also said the following at a breakfast meeting with the fellows: "I love mentoring. There is no politics in mentoring. You just have to be nice." My classmates and I still remember these words today. Professor Hong gave us so much attention and encouragement before he retired that I also had the same desire to become a good mentor.

The parable of the talents can be found in Matthew 25. It tells of a master who gives his three servants five talents, two talents, and one talent, respectively. One talent was equivalent to twenty years' worth of their salary. The servants who received five and two talents each put their talents to work and made a profit. However, the servant who received one talent buried it in the ground and returned it to the master when he came back home.

Today, "talent" could be interpreted as our capacity for success. For that reason, this story is not as easily understood as the parable of the vineyard I shared earlier. It sounds like a story about the rich and the poor. While praying one day, I suddenly realized that "talents" could be nothing other than "wounds" or "past hardships." The reason we pay close attention to Helen Keller's story is that she showed incredible talent despite the hardships she experienced. The more talents you have, the more mission fields you are able to serve.

In my case, the scars caused by losing my mentors gave me the passion to become a good mentor myself. Every wound

Keyword 3

on my heart gave me another "talent." Just as the Five Holy Wounds, including the nail piercings of Jesus, have become a sign of glory, I pray that my pain may become a talent—the ability to empathize with other souls and to love them.

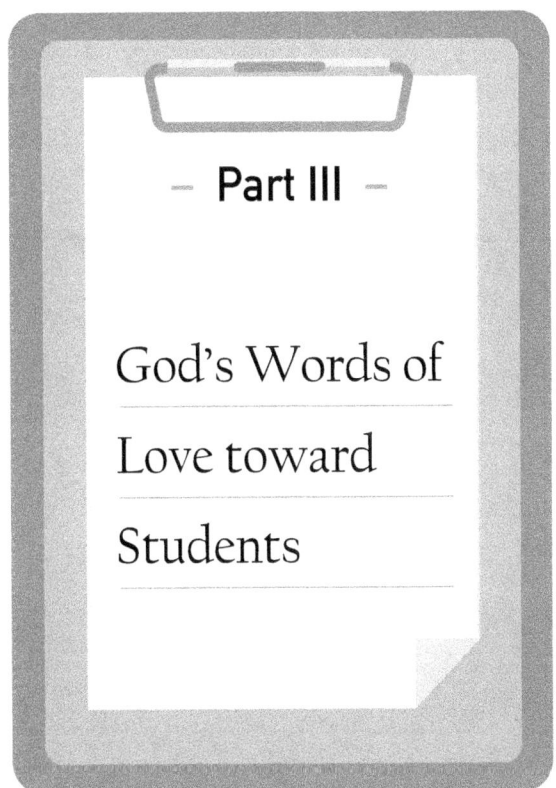

Part III

God's Words of Love toward Students

Perfect Timing

Don't Let My Will Get in the Way

I had never imagined I would end up living in Chicago. It was a whole new experience when I started applying for professor positions at various university hospitals in Houston. I thought to myself, *Finally, after a long period of training, I'm going to secure a position.* I wanted to go where God wanted me to be. Of course, I had my preferences, like a place with prestigious hospitals, excellent mentors, good weather and natural surroundings, a great place to educate my children, and direct flights to Korea, among other things. However, I believed that God knew better than me about where I should be.

I thought about the experiences I'd had with God in Baltimore, where He saw my family as one entity rather than just me. I had the conviction that God would lead us to the best place for all of us. So, I prayed in this way: *Even if a place seems perfect and desirable, don't let my will get in the way, God. Have Your way.*

Can I Pray for You?

In the United States, fellows usually receive offers one year or even as early as two years before graduation. Usually, an outline of where to go starts to emerge about a year before graduation. However, in my case, despite having interviews in multiple places and even second-round interviews, there was no opportunity that came my way as my graduation approached. I was the only one among my peers who hadn't signed a new job contract. I started to worry about graduating without a job waiting for me because it would mean the end of insurance coverage for my wife and three children. While I was waiting endlessly, I regretted for a moment that I had asked God to stop my will from getting in His way.

I couldn't understand why every road was being blocked for seemingly no reason. My self-esteem was affected. I felt humiliated and sorry for my family. I resented God for keeping me anxious until the very last minute.

However, even if God's timing in my heart was different from my own timing, even if it felt much slower, there was an indescribable sense of anticipation for God's work. Therefore, I decided to wait patiently in expectation. It was perhaps due to this expectation that I was able to withstand the long waiting period.

During that time, I coincidentally stumbled across an opening for a clinical trial coordinator position at Northwestern University Hospital in Chicago. Surprisingly, I received a formal offer right after the initial interview, and the next day, I decided to accept the position officially. Dramatically, just one month before graduating from my residency program in

June, I secured the job, and I could start working immediately in July. I also quickly found a place to move into. Since I couldn't move right away, I stayed at the dormitory offered by the KOSTA Conference, a Midwest Coast Conference held at Wheaton University near Chicago, with my car and minimal belongings. That was how my life in Chicago began.

Although I hadn't specifically prayed to go to Chicago, I could trust that all these processes were unfolding under the guidance of God, who knows me even better than I know myself. I was excited about my upcoming life in Chicago.

God's Plan Is Perfect

Even the current position I am in was due to my following a path I had no knowledge of at all. Currently, I am directing numerous frontline clinical trials and patient research that takes place at the Lurie Cancer Center of Northwestern University. Less than a year after becoming a professor, I became one of the responsible individuals for the precision medicine MATCH clinical trial conducted by the National Cancer Institute (NCI). Around the same time, I also became one of the co-principal investigators responsible for planning and managing a nationwide immunotherapy clinical trial for rare cancers within the U.S. clinical trial group SWOG. These groundbreaking opportunities likely would not have been possible if I had gone to another university hospital. All of these felt like another "surprise gift" from God.

Even in Korea, where I had left, my research was recognized. In 2016, I was selected as an international authority in the field of precision medicine, and I gave a keynote presentation at the Fiftieth Anniversary World Science and Technology Congress organized by the Korea Federation of Science and Technology Societies (KOFST). In 2020, I also received the Dean's Award, an academic award presented at the SNU School of Medicine Alumni Association in the United States.

Great relationships were among the many other gifts from God I received. First of all, God allowed me to meet many excellent collaborators whom I had never met before. He gave me opportunities for mentorship within the clinical trial society. Through these societies, He also granted me the privilege of making wonderful connections.

Furthermore, even when I lived in Baltimore, Philadelphia, and Houston, I used to drive or take a fourteen-hour flight to attend the Midwest Coast Conference, but now I can easily attend the conference with just an hour's drive. Here, I can serve and meet fellow workers of faith abundantly.

Moreover, due to Chicago's central location in the United States, many important conferences and meetings are held here, considering participants from both the East and West Coasts. There have been more than a few occasions when I felt God's guidance in connecting me with many people while living here.

Taking care of patients, teaching disciples, and conducting cancer research in Chicago brings me great gratitude and happiness. I am particularly thankful for the disciples who come to my research lab without me seeking them out. Seeing the unexpected positive results of the projects I created for my disciples, I witness God's work.

I love the praise song "More Than I Could Ask or Imagine": "More than I could ask or imagine,/ You will answer, O Lord./ More than I could think or comprehend,/ You will accomplish, O Lord." Just as these lyrics proclaim, God's work goes beyond my prayers and imagination, and now I am starting to anticipate it little by little. It is difficult when all I see is blocked paths. God will block anything that is not His will, but if it is where He wants me to be, I have faith that He will use me in His timing and His way.

Young Kwang, I Entrust Them in Your Care

People Are the Land of God

There is a well-known children's fairy tale called "The Little Princess." Sarah Crewe is the main character of the story. Her father, a successful businessman in India, sends her to a boarding school after her mother's early passing. Sarah lives like a princess at the school, but when news reaches her that her father has passed away and left her with no inheritance, she suddenly finds herself in rags, living in the attic as a servant. Despite the difficult circumstances, Sarah continues to behave "like a princess"—with resilience. At a decisive moment, Tom Carrisford, a friend of her father, comes to find her to deliver the inheritance left by her father, enabling her to live "like a princess" once again.

One day while praying, God reminded me of this fairy tale, which I had seen when I was young. The first thing I realized was that Sarah's confident attitude toward life seemed like the attitude I should have as a child of God. It felt like

Sarah was reminding me that no matter how difficult and challenging my position in life might be, I should remember that I am a child who inherits the Kingdom. Occasionally, I still read the dialogue that Sarah spoke to the headmistress of the boarding school: "I am a princess. As are all other girls. Even if they live in a tiny attic. Even if they are clad in rags, not pretty, not clever, nor young. They are all princesses."

The next thing I realized was that the role God has given me is similar to the role of "Tom," Sarah's father's friend. Tom delivers Sarah not his own inheritance, but her father's.

In John 15:15 (NIV), Jesus says "I have called you friends." I realized that although I am a child of God, I also think of myself as His friend. The thought arose in me to be a friend like "Tom," a true father figure, to other "Sarahs," the true children of God, and to share His love and blessings with them. Then I saw many "Sarahs" around me who strive not to lose hope amidst countless desperate situations. Could they be the rightful heirs to the abundant inheritance God has prepared for them? And perhaps I am in a position right now, in my research lab and clinic in Chicago, where I should seek out these "Sarahs" and fulfill the role of "Tom, a friend of their father."

Love from Above

I once encountered the challenging assignment of undertaking a clinical observership in Miami, Florida, prior to my relocation to the United States following my military service.

Can I Pray for You?

Given that I had not graduated from a medical school in the United States, and I lacked familiarity with the American health-care system, it was imperative for me to gain practical experience within a U.S. hospital in order to pursue residency training programs in the country.

I distinctly recall sending numerous emails to hospitals where I hoped to gain observational experience. Regrettably, there were no invitations extended, and the majority of professors remained unresponsive. I felt utterly adrift. Fortunately, I eventually discovered a program in Miami that granted me the opportunity to observe and procure recommendation letters. Going through this process enlightened me to the challenges faced by individuals commencing their journey in a foreign land, devoid of familial, community, or academic connections.

Today, I find myself on the receiving end of such emails, often originating from places like Pakistan or Brazil. In Matthew 25:40 (NIV), Jesus imparts this wisdom: "Whatever you did for one of the least of these brothers and sisters of mine, you did for me." Within a hospital context, the "least of these" resembles inexperienced students or observers quietly standing in the shadows. Sometime after assuming the role of an attending physician, I began to view these emails as requests from God, akin to those made by a friend.

Here is My son. Here is My daughter. Young Kwang, I entrust them into your care, God's voice echoed softly in my heart. As someone who cannot deny that God has directly guided me to this position, I want to fulfill the role of "Tom"

Young Kwang, I Entrust Them in Your Care

for them. This is why, among my mentees at my lab and clinic in Chicago, I have not only undergraduate or medical students, residents, and fellows, but also other students and doctors without any connections in the United States who have set out to learn clinical medicine and cancer research. Although I didn't know them, their emails found me.

I have only been on a few international mission trips, but precious souls from the mission fields in India, Azerbaijan, Syria, etc., have come to me in the form of disciples.

To be honest, it was not easy teaching these mentees who had no clinical or research experience in the United States. For someone like me, who had little patience, it was a test of character. My work received no recognition from the hospital or the school. Nevertheless, I started serving them in my research lab in Chicago, trusting that they were sent by God. The reason I sincerely hoped for and supported their success was simply because God loved them. When I prayed for them, God poured out genuine compassion in my heart for them.

There is a Korean phrase that translates: "love flowing down." During medical school, I was a member of a classic guitar club called Arpeggio. Within the club, we created many wonderful memories. Seniors used to say, "If we buy you a meal, make sure to treat the juniors who come after you." That is what "love flowing down" meant, they said. Likewise, I tell my mentees that what I want from them is for them to help others who later need their help. That is the life not of paying back, but of paying forward.

Can I Pray for You?

Luke 14:13 (NIV) tells us to take an extra step to invite those who may not pay us back. Jesus tells us to intentionally invite the poor, the crippled, and the blind into the Kingdom.

To someone like me who likes tennis, it sounded as if God wanted me to strike an ace serve—a serve that precisely targets the corner and cannot be returned by the opponent. God, who rejoices in a serve that cannot be returned or a service that cannot be repaid, says that only you can pay back. Jesus says: "Give, and it will be given to you. A good measure, pressed down, shaken together and running over, will be poured into your lap. For with the measure you use, it will be measured to you" (Luke 6:38 NIV). Listening to God's heart is the foundation of my ministry. This is when I wrote the poem "A Request" from my heart.

A Request

by
Young Kwang Chae

In the morning, I receive a request from God:
Take good care of My son.
Take good care of My daughter.

During the day, I see God's heart:
My heart aches because of My son.
I shed many tears because of My daughter.

In the evening, I hear God's voice:
Thank you for waiting on My son.
Thank you for embracing My daughter.

Who am I that He should ask me?
Grace that is freely gifted to me,
An infinitely blessed life.
I yearn to hear every day
The Source of my empathy,
God's request.

Keyword 4

Listening: a ministry begins with listening

I am fond of a poem called "A Visitor" by Hyeonjong Jung. The poet says:

> That a person is coming
> Is in fact an enormous thing
> That's because the person
> The person's past
> The person's present
> And the person's future all comes together
> Because a person's life in its entirety is coming
> Easy to break
> Thus maybe broken
> Soul is coming.

Through my counseling ministry at KOSTA retreats, I understood at least in part what it is like to have a person's life and his or her broken soul come to me. I also thought about how to invite those souls.

Listening with all your heart for a time as short as an hour and twenty minutes is truly important. So whomever

Keyword 4

I talk with in that moment I only look into the person's eyes and listen with all my heart.

This is also why I decided not to look at the screen while seeing a patient in the clinic. I write the necessary information on a piece of paper that I can refer to, and then I look in the patient's eyes from the beginning to the end. It is because I want to focus on the smallest of changes in facial expression and the flow of his or her soul.

While this way of seeing patients takes more time, since I have to write out notes and put in orders after interviewing the patient, I focus on my patients during the clinic, thinking that it is not just a disease, but a person's life that is coming through the door. This is the same way I approach my mentees.

What is truly surprising is that even though I cannot provide an answer, as long as I listen enough and pray for my patient, God steps in and completes His work. To be honest, there is no answer that I can provide with my own wisdom. One mentee told me that I was the first person to be curious about her own thoughts. Another time, when I was counseling at KOSTA, a mentee told me that looking back on what happened in her life, God did not seem to exist. I later heard that the very next day, he was praising the Lord again. I only listened, and God did His work.

Listening forms the foundation of all the ministry in which I am involved. When "the person's life in its entirety is coming," as the poet Hyeonjong Jung said, we are tasked

Keyword 4 ....

with listening closely and drawing the person's "life curve" so that we can get to know his or her life better. I believe that healing starts when there is someone who listens to your story full-heartedly.

That God is always listening to my story and my prayers more than anyone else is my source of huge comfort.

Unexpected Proposal: Ten-Minute Morning Prayer

An Unexpected Suggestion: Shall We Pray Together?

One day, I received an unexpected email. A physician from Korea asked me if he could come to my lab in Chicago and learn from me. He had heard about me because his older sister was a friend of my wife's at church. He told me that during his prayers, he felt that God wanted him to go to Chicago to meet me. His older sister happened to be working as a physician in Baltimore at that time, so I replied that it would be better for him to travel to Baltimore rather than Chicago. However, he consistently expressed his interest in Chicago and eventually ended up coming to my lab there.

The day after he arrived, he told me, "Dr. Chae, would you like to pray with me in the morning?" He told me that he wanted to pray with me before going into the clinic. I was perplexed. It was uncomfortable to have someone you don't know very well to ask to pray with you and say that God Himself would also want this. I told him that I would pray about his suggestion. In my prayers, I felt that it would not be bad to pray for just ten minutes together. I usually arrived at my lab at 6:40 a.m. So, we met every morning at 6:40 a.m. and prayed for ten minutes together. He would pray out loud in tongues and occasionally pour out his tears.

Every morning, I was naturally able to pray more for the patients and their families I would see each day, as well as for my mentees. While I didn't realize it in the beginning, I came to look forward to what God had planned to do through me thanks to these morning prayers. Even when I was away at a conference or working remotely, I scheduled online meetings to continue my prayers. I learned little by little through prayer what it is to overcome situations that challenge your soul. A medical school professor who came to visit my lab participated in our prayer meetings even when the doctor who first suggested the idea returned to Korea. The morning prayers have continued even to this day, with mentees who have come to learn from me. I hear stories of how some of my mentees have continued this ritual back in Korea every single day to this day. I believe that spirituality must become a habit. We carry on the tradition even now through book clubs or testimony meetings.

Pray Specifically and Individually

Whenever we have these ten-minute prayer meetings, we ask for any urgent or important prayer requests from mentees. The more specific these requests are, the better.

Unexpected Proposal: Ten-Minute Morning Prayer

You can see crystal clear that our God is a living God when He replies to the specific prayers we make. Back when I was younger, I used to ask my father to buy me a present; I did not just want a nice present, but I asked for a specific item at a specific store. Throughout my life, I have made many prayers where I told the Lord I wanted to experience the living God through His answers to my specific prayers. My wife and I came up with a ridiculous idea, where we prayed for our first child's birthday to fall exactly on our requested date, so that we could experience how God answers our specific requests and be His witnesses. We even prayed for a specific time for her labor to start. God answered our prayers on the exact day and at the exact time.

On another occasion, I prayed for my sister's wedding date. My wife and I wanted to celebrate her wedding during our next visit to Korea, when I needed to change my visa prior to starting residency since I would be too busy to make another trip while training. I began to pray that my sister would get married on a specific date, when she did not even have a partner at that time. Shortly afterward, my sister found a partner, and they ended up getting married on exactly the day I had requested of the Lord. Of course, I did not tell anybody that I was praying for that date. The wedding was originally scheduled on a different date, but the wedding hall had to reschedule it. What is more surprising is that my sister's now-husband had also been praying for two years to marry in the month of May.

Can I Pray for You?

I advise my mentees to pray specifically. Recently, one of my mentees specifically told the Lord that she would like to get trained in Chicago and live in that city. She was getting nervous as she received her invitation late in the interview season and had scheduling issues. After much anxiety, she thankfully managed to secure an interview and eventually was pre-matched to her dream residency program.

Likewise, another mentee who could not find a residency position for two consecutive years prayed that if she got just one interview, she would take that as God's sign and not give up. Lo and behold, she received one interview offer. She felt encouraged and thoroughly prepared for the interview. While she did not match to that hospital, she soon got another offer from a higher-ranking hospital and matched there.

Both mentees discovered what they truly wanted and where they wanted to get trained. Although God might not answer every specific prayer, if He does, you will get to see His meticulous work.

Unexpected Proposal: Morning Book Club

An Unexpected Suggestion: "Let's Do a Book Club"

I was receiving emails from physicians all over the world. My inbox was soon overloaded with emails that expressed a desire to come and learn from me. Among them was one from Ramon Checo, who used to work as physician in the Dominican Republic and has since moved to the United States. His wife had already started her training at a U.S. hospital, but he had failed to match on his first attempt. While he was making his second attempt, he found his way to my lab.

To train as a resident in a U.S. hospital, physicians must go through a process called "the match." First, you are screened for an interview based on your supporting documents. Once the interview season is over, you rank your programs in order of preference and upload the rank list to the Match. Likewise, the programs upload their rank list of applicants they interviewed. The system then matches each applicant with a single hospital. In March, the Match first announces whether an applicant has successfully matched to a program. A few days later, it reveals the name of the program.

However, Ramon did not match even on his second try. He sent me a text message saying, "Dr. Chae, I am in panic. I don't know what to do." I had never received such a text message from a mentee before, so I felt lost. I told him to get some rest first and read some books. He asked me for a book recommendation, and I suggested Pastor Rick Warren's *The Purpose Driven Life*. This book came to mind because it had played a big role when I was trying to see the big picture as a medical student.

A few days later, Ramon contacted me again. He told me he had found a Spanish translation of that book at his parents' house, and he had already finished it. He then made an unexpected suggestion: "Dr. Chae, I would like to do a book club with this book." *What a bold fellow,* I thought. But how could I do a book club with him in the midst of my hectic day at the hospital when I had to prepare to see patients from early morning until late at night?

I turned to God and prayed. Then it occurred to me that since the book had forty chapters, I could make time for an hour each Friday before the clinic to go through one chapter. As I had found profound grace in this book and felt indebted to it, I decided to host a book club every Friday at 6:40 a.m. in the patient consult room.

The Book Club Becomes the Stepping-Stone of My Ministry

When I first started this book club, I did not know how many mentees would meet God for the first time or return to God through our meetings. I believed that God was involved in starting the ten-minute prayers and book club in Chicago, as He had started the prayer meetings during my residency and fellowship.

I have a scripture from the Bible that I want to share along with this thought: "For it is God who works in you to will and to act in order to fulfill his good purpose" (Philippians 2:13 NIV).

God inspires me with new ideas, such as starting the prayer meeting or the book club. Through these experiences, I came to believe that my role was to obey God when He would let me know what He wanted me to do.

Recently, I heard good news about a former mentee, Ramon. The news came during my testimony in a meeting with the Global Medical Missions Alliance (GMMA), where I currently serve as a mentor for the Northwestern Chapter. A cardiac surgeon mentor recognized Ramon's photo on my slides and told me that he was working as an intern at his hospital. Ramon and I got in touch again, and he sent me pictures with his lovely daughter. He said the GMMA mentor had invited him to a Bible study group at his hospital. It is always joyful to witness God's hand at work.

The book club became a space for my mentees from all around the world, including Azerbaijan, Saudi Arabia,

Pakistan, India, and Brazil, to share their lives with one another. Despite coming from different religious backgrounds—including atheism, Islam, Hinduism, Catholicism, and Protestantism, to name a few—I could empathize with them and pray for them as they were living in uncertainty. Looking back, our time together was precious.

Then came the COVID-19 pandemic, and we could no longer gather together in person. My mentees and I instead participated in book clubs virtually at the request of students in the GMMA Northwestern Chapter. This book club was an important platform through which my life mission to "make the lives of others successful" was realized. Various people were connected through the book club, including my mentees from Korea who had joined my lab and a Ph.D. who was doing research at a medical school. The book club lives on to this day, and I use it as a space where anyone who has gone through my clinic and lab can visit comfortably, especially when they have a prayer request. I always thank the Lord for giving me the privilege to witness how He works in each of our lives through the book club.

A Cameo Life Starring Friendship

Hearing Testimonies as Beautiful as Flowers

I learn a lot through my mentees' life stories. Whenever I see my mentees bear the weight of their lives, I think of how burdensome our lives can be. However, I also frequently observe how they become closer to God during their time in Chicago; they leave with a sense of peace that the world cannot understand.

One of the questions I often ask my mentees is, "When was the hardest time in your life?" One mentee answered, "Right now"; he had not heard back from any of the hospitals during the interview season. Despite his low scores and the lack of offers, he said he was not nervous due to his connection with God and the Scriptures. He finally received a single interview, and he matched to that university hospital program that only accepted U.S. medical school graduates. There were other mentees who came to Chicago with high hopes for success and life in the United States. As time went by, they experienced what it was like to live with God and testified that they could rejoice and be peaceful in the Lord, regardless of their match results. Their testimonies were as beautiful as the flowers that have grown from the seeds of the Gospel.

One mentee opened up her heart to God out of curiosity. She was touched by the friendships of Christians and watched how other mentees' lives had changed after meeting God. Mentees who identified themselves as Christians prayed for the salvation of those who had just met God or who had not yet met Him. Together, the mentees laughed, cried, and endured hard times.

Rain or shine, only God can make flowers bloom. I am thankful to God, who has called upon each one of us as flowers and allowed us to bloom.

Take Your Cues from God

I shared a story about cameos during my medical mission trip to Mexico with GMMA. I was concerned that many students seemed to be envious of other students and idolizing lives that looked good on the outside. I also saw students who tried to please God but ended up feeling hurt because they were afraid of infringing on someone else's life. My concerns led me to think about cameo appearances in movies and realize that our role was to be a cameo in others' lives.

A Cameo Life Starring Friendship

Sometimes a big-name actor would star as a cameo following a request from the director. Even though the actor plays a minor role, it does not affect their pride. They have chosen to star in the movie, not because of the size of the role, but because of his or her friendship with the director. Even if the other members of the crew do not recognize the actor and think of the actor as playing a minor role, the actor does not care. That is because the actor is confident about the lead role he or she plays in other movies.

We all live as the lead actor in a movie that is our lives. Sometimes we make a cameo appearance when a director asks. The only reason we would do so is that we are close with God, who is the Director of all our lives. According to the Director's signals and orders, we enter a movie that is another person's life, and then we exit once we have done our part. Since we are not playing the lead actor, we do not complain, nor are we in a rush. We are not affected by how big our role is or whether we influence the ending. We simply believe in the Director and carry out our minor role. There is no envy, sadness, disappointment, or regret.

Every day, I make a cameo appearance in another person's life. This is because I love God only. My day begins with receiving a new role and script from God. As a cameo, I dream of adding value to each life that I encounter.

Flower

by
Young Kwang Chae

Flower is a flower
Not because it is pretty
Nor because it dazzles.

Not because it is fragrant,
Nor because the bees come searching.

Not because it knows the seasons,
Nor because it blooms.

You have always been a flower
Ever since you were a seed
Ever since the beginning of time.

You are my one and only flower
You are a flower
Because I love you.

Keyword 5

Celebration: a sense of encouragement and recognition

I have seen mentees who had never known about Jesus, or had distanced themselves from Him, accept Jesus as their Lord as they spent time in my lab. Naturally, we thought it would be appropriate to throw parties to celebrate their "spiritual birthday." There were also mentees who felt for the first time that they wanted to talk about Jesus to others, and for these mentees, we awarded them with a "Certificate of Discipleship" to celebrate their new lives as Jesus' disciples.

We also gathered together to celebrate mentees' last day at work. We shared our memories with them by making videos from recorded messages and photos we took together. We filmed these memories in hopes that they would look back on this phase of their lives when they had spent time with God, just as a married couple would reminisce about the past while watching their wedding videos. Through these efforts, I could feel that God was finding my ministry of celebration and making memories joyful.

Can I Pray for You?

In Luke 15:6 (NIV), Jesus "calls his friends and neighbors together and says, 'Rejoice with me.'" Jesus enjoyed celebrating with others and knew it was central to His ministry. In John 21, after Jesus has risen from the dead, He appears in front of the disciples at the Sea of Galilee early in the morning and feeds them bread and fish. Paul the apostle states in Romans 12:15 to "rejoice with those who rejoice; mourn with those who mourn" (NIV).

I like to imagine what Jesus would look like as a party planner. It is telling that the first miracle of Jesus happened at a wedding party in Cana. Perhaps He performed this miracle to liven up the party? Before I knew it, I was trying to imitate Jesus as a party planner, imagining how He would love ministries in which I host parties and celebrate with others.

God said we will receive a prize in the future and that we should look forward to that prize. Hebrews 11:6 says, "And without faith it is impossible to please God, because anyone who comes to him must believe that he exists and that he rewards those who earnestly seek him" (NIV).

We as humans need recognition, from whomever that recognition may come. Maybe that is why the Bible has so many verses that tell us to encourage and recognize each other. One time, a student did an observership at my clinic for a month. It was a Black student who would peek shyly over my shoulder to observe. That student and the student's parents later sent me a glass trophy that read "Gratitude Award" for showing the model example of kindness and leadership. I had never received an award from a high school student

Keyword 5

before. But that token of gratitude was that I had decided to act as I had learned. Every year, I create glass trophies that prize gratitude and service for any of my mentees who have displayed exceptional service in the lab. As I see mentees who are overjoyed by receiving the trophy, I imagine how happy I would be receiving a prize directly from God. Much less than a trophy, a word of encouragement from God would suffice. I am reminded of a phrase in the K-Drama Hospital Playlist in which Kim, Daemyung, who stars as an obstetrician, says to a resident: "You did really well today." I think that would be enough.

Ongoing Relay of Testimonies in the Lab

Testimony Relay Becomes a Ministry

Once the ten-minute prayers became a part of life at the lab, I wanted my lab mentees to know how it had all started. The best way to do that, I thought, would be to invite the mentee who had first suggested the idea to give a testimony. Because he was in Korea and we were in the United States, we scheduled a Zoom meeting for him to share his testimony. We had a higher turnout than expected. It was a great opportunity to have so many former mentees and current mentees be in the same space together. I wondered how nice it would be to continue to share with my mentees the invaluable life stories of other physicians I know. This is how the ministry of "testimony relay" began. We hold testimony meetings almost every week.

During this span of an hour and twenty minutes, we first pray for the testimony itself and for any urgent or important

Ongoing Relay of Testimonies in the Lab

prayer topics, and then we listen to the testimony and finish with a Q&A session. This has touched so many lives, and my mentees look forward to this time of the week.

My mentees reported feeling a sense of community during the Q&A sessions when they learned that others had similar worries or went through similar challenges. Some mentees even said they found their purpose in life after listening to the testimonies by the GMMA mentors. While preparing his testimony, one mentee was able to come to terms with the confusion and disappointment he had with God after a sudden death in his family. New connections formed between the mentees and the mentors, leading to follow-up meetings. A friend from my medical school graduating class who is currently attending a medical school in New York shared his "Fail CV" with us, showing us how God led his life despite many failures. Everyone participating in these meetings—from the speakers to the listeners—made an extra leap in their personal growth.

I thought about whether we have opportunities like this as adults in which we learn about someone's life in such detail. In the speakers' perspectives, I wondered if the speakers could share all the ups and downs of life to others anywhere else. The Q&A sessions create a space for mentors and mentees to exchange compliments. It is always heartwarming to watch them encourage each other.

Bearing the Fruit of Grace

One mentee thought this ministry would end after just a few testimonies. She did not think there would be people who could serve as role models and share their stories under God's grace. To her surprise, a number of former lab members and mentors agreed to testify on our platform. Volunteers followed one after the other, as one would see potatoes pop up as one pulled on the roots. One mentor invited another mentor to testify, and they would all become mentors for the lab members. Looking back, my planning brought these people to my lab. That is why I am still excited about the testimony meetings, where I can look forward to the next person whom God will send my way.

An All-Line That Doesn't Sleep

A Surprise Gift Called Bible Study

Missionary Tae-hoon Kim, who had participated in our testimony relay, contacted me one day out of the blue. Dr. Kim, who is the author of the book *The Broken Plate*, is also a senior from my medical school. After years of working as a liver transplant surgeon in Korea, he was dispatched as a missionary to Ethiopia, where he trained future physicians at the Ethiopian Ministry of Health.

While I did not know him personally, he was spending his sabbatical in Los Angeles when I reached out to him, and he graciously agreed to share his testimony with our group. I was very excited to have him in our testimony meeting because I was moved by the testimony he gave during the Daniel Prayer Meeting.

After Dr. Kim got to meet the members at my lab through Zoom, he made an offer to lead a weekly Bible study group with the current and former lab members. I was so thankful.

Can I Pray for You?

He made his offer at a timely moment when I had a strong desire to read the Bible and reflect on its message.

We scheduled weekly Wednesday Zoom sessions called *Walking Together with the Gospel of John*, when we would study the gospel of John. It was a truly fruitful time, during which not only my lab mentees participated, but many other people did as well, including mentors who had testified. With His grace, this weekly meeting continues to this day, having moved on to other books in the Bible.

Dr. Kim expressed his intent to meet my mentees in Chicago, and he came for a six-day trip from LA with Missionary Choong-guk Lee of Cambodia. It was as if Chicago had become a mission site. The two missionaries met my mentees one by one, listening to their stories and answering their questions with all their hearts. Through these conversations, my mentees were able to picture life in the mission field and grow closer to God.

Another missionary, Mr. Kwan-Tae Park, who is serving in Mongolia and is the author of the book *The Hand of God*, also visited our lab during his sabbatical. He counseled my mentees and shared with them invaluable stories of how he gave up his career as a pancreatic transplant surgeon at Korea University Hospital to go to the Mongolian Mission Hospital. My heart was once again filled with gratitude.

It was my first time spending extended periods of time with missionaries. I was taken aback at God's grace; it wasn't me who had planned all this. God had sent these missionaries to Chicago and used them to allow me and my mentees to understand His Word.

Online Ministry That Transcends Generations and Continents

I was hosting book clubs on Zoom even before the COVID-19 pandemic; I wanted my undergraduate students living far away from my office to participate in our meetings. My ministry has since followed a hybrid online/offline model. And just as I began to move other meetings online, the pandemic struck. Because everyone had the option to join online, all these ministries could continue without interruption, as if we had prepared for the pandemic before it existed!

Even now, people all over the world—including Seoul, Thailand, Morocco, New York, Chicago, LA, Nashville, and Iowa City, to name a few—join in on our meetings. Those who cannot make it to the live meetings can watch the recorded videos online.

Even those who had never visited my lab began to participate in our online research meetings, testimony meetings, and book clubs. Despite the global shutdown, ironically we had more people than ever sharing our research, testimonies, and reading experiences. Needless to say, I was surprised and thankful that even though the pandemic made offline meetings difficult, our online ministry was experiencing a revival. While other hospital clinics and labs were closing their doors, we had more mentees joining my lab and participating online. Many mentors working at university hospitals also partook in our online ministry. Thanks to the service of physicians who volunteered as mentors and the participation of students and mentees joining from all over the world, the online ministry could transcend generations and continents despite the pandemic.

Even Make Academic Conference Trips Different

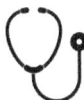

Life Like a Retreat

Back when I attended a church retreat in college, I prayed, *God, please make my daily life like a retreat.* At the retreat, I was entirely focused on God; I shared stories with other attendees, and we would even challenge each other's faith and pray for one another. When I returned home, I noticed that nothing had changed in my daily life, and I lived with disappointment.

Now, on my way home from work, I mutter to myself, "Oh, this prayer has been answered." As a professor, I begin my days praying for all my patients and mentees and discussing life with my mentees through a book club. I am, indeed, living life like I'm at a retreat. God's grace has been slowly but faithfully changing the rigid, stubborn person that I am.

While working at a university hospital, cancer societies and conferences are times I look forward to, as these are academic meetings where I can present my research and learn the latest information in the field of oncology. In the past, I wondered why I would need to memorize so many names of medications, but now I am in a position to cheer when a groundbreaking study or clinical trial results of new drugs are released at the conference. As I treat patients and live my life as a cancer researcher, I even feel that the current rate of new drug development is slow. Another favorite part about attending conferences is the joy of meeting people from all over the world; I enjoy discussing questions with them and getting new ideas from their work.

God creates time and space for life-sharing during these academic gatherings. In cancer research workshops held in Colorado, I met a few co-workers of faith, and we spent every morning praying and reflecting on God's Word. While we came together as researchers, we were His children in the mornings, reading the Bible together and sharing tears.

We called our morning gathering the "conference revival meeting." We put aside time in the morning to update and reflect on each other's faith journey. Thanks to our friendship, some of the members have agreed to serve as mentors for many ministries in our lab.

Experience Spiritual Recovery at a Conference

The first time I attended a conference retreat with my mentees it was in Washington, D.C. We were there for an annual conference on cancer immunotherapy. I fondly remember praying with them and sharing our life stories

Even Make Academic Conference Trips Different

during the retreat. Since then, I have held revival meetings with my co-workers and students during conferences. During the COVID-19 pandemic, we met online instead. Because I was feeling emotionally disconnected in the middle of the pandemic, I could feel God's grace in a much deeper sense. Revival meetings at the World Lung Cancer Society conference, which was held in various places like Yokohama and Barcelona, also led to His grace and spiritual recovery.

One of my mentees who was working in the South Korean military as a public health doctor came to Barcelona to present a lung cancer treatment marker study, which he had performed under my guidance. When I prayed with him on the phone after the conference, I could not erase the thought that *God loves this person so much*. I kept crying while praying for his blessings. It was very special for me to see God's work and experience His love through these cancer societies.

Keyword 6

Character: a good teacher is seen in life

Sometimes I could tell what my mentees were thinking. Some were trying to cut corners; others just wanted to get the job done as quickly as possible without showing any hint of enthusiasm. My first reactions when I noticed these kinds of attitudes were anger and resentment. When a mentee was struggling with English, I thought to myself, *He's going to have trouble communicating with his patients.* When a mentee was struggling with scientific writing, I was quick to judge and compare, even though I had been in their shoes early in my career. I had to admit that I did not have the characteristics of a good mentor.

A few years ago, two of my mentees told me that I did not seem to have any love and that I "looked scary." I was shocked. After giving it some thought, I realized that I had placed my passions for research ahead of any consideration for my mentees. I was obsessed with power, achievement, and worldliness. Although I had the desire to be recognized as a good researcher and a good mentor in God's eyes, I lacked empathy in my day-to-day life.

Keyword 6

God changed me. By helping me to see the extent of my limitations at every moment, God made me acknowledge my mistakes before Him and seek His righteous guidance. Years later, the mentee who had told me I lacked love returned to my lab for an away elective. Remarkably, this time he said I seemed to be "living like Jesus."

I was so glad that God had been guiding my development of Jesus' character in my life. I realized that I had to be changed under the guidance of Jesus, sometimes through listening to feedback from the people around me, and sometimes from my mentees.

Up until that day, I had only noticed one aspect of God's work—God using me to mold and transform my mentees. I started to see that God also had been using my research ministry to mold and transform the loveless person that I was. One of my favorite phrases is "Character is fruit." To this day, I wish to present my character as fruit, shamelessly, to God.

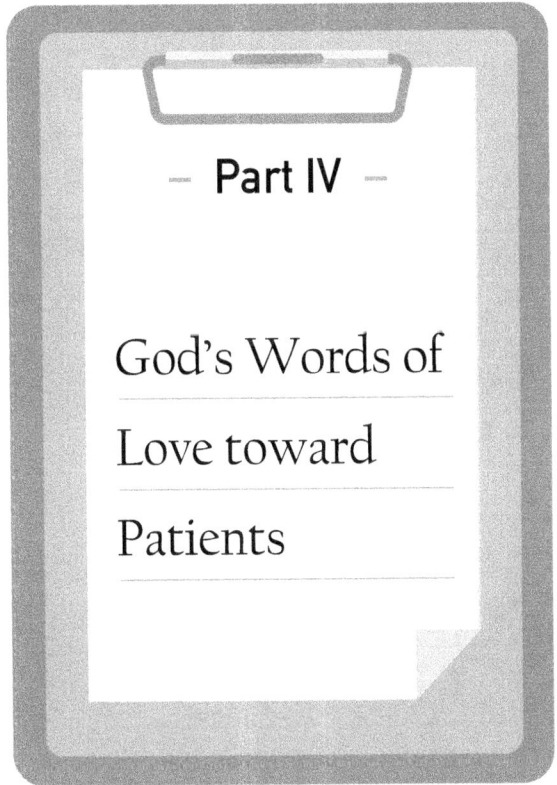

Part IV

God's Words of Love toward Patients

A Patient's Prayer That Teared Me Up

Waiting for Prayer

During my time as an internist at the Philadelphia Albert Einstein Medical Center, I had a memorable encounter with a Black patient who was suffering from terminal kidney failure. He had developed blood clots due to an infection, and these clots had spread to his veins, heart valves, and brain. Despite his deteriorating condition, he expressed the desire to be placed in hospice care. Unfortunately, he had to endure another week in the internal medicine ward due to various insurance issues that hindered his transfer. I remained his doctor until my last day in the internal medicine ward, and it was emotionally challenging to witness his prolonged wait, especially with another critically ill patient under my care.

On a different day, while attending to a patient in the hemodialysis room, a nurse and an intern abruptly left the room in response to urgent calls. This left just me and this Black male patient alone in the room. Although he initially appeared distant, I felt a strong urge to offer a prayer for him. I knelt down beside him and held his hand, looking into his eyes. I asked, "Sir, can I pray for you?" He looked at me, puzzled, then gave his consent with a nod.

With newfound courage, I began to pray, "God, my patient is very ill, so please watch over him and grant him peace until his last day. Bestow faith upon him, and I believe that we will reunite in heaven." I could sense the depth of his emotions. It felt as if God was telling me, *Young Kwang, I've been waiting for this moment to share My love through you. That's why the patient hasn't been sent to hospice yet and remains on your patient list.* I was deeply moved by God's love, and my voice trembled with emotion throughout the prayer. I shed tears as I prayed for an extended period, and when I eventually opened my eyes, I saw that the patient was also crying.

I pondered why God had chosen me as a conduit for His love, especially considering my previous discomfort with expressing myself in front of others. I had initially pursued the path of studying for the U.S. medical license exams and becoming a doctor in the United States based on my own will. However, it occurred to me that the Lord had been preparing me for this moment all along, allowing me to meet this patient precisely when he needed a Christian presence in his life.

Now it is my Turn

A similar transformative experience occurred at the Northwestern Memorial Hospital, where I work. A White

A Patient's Prayer That Teared Me Up

elderly patient, fatigued from chemotherapy, required hospitalization and a pause in therapy to regain her strength. As I had been accompanying her throughout her cancer journey, I felt a deep sense of empathy for her. During one of our rounds, I mustered the courage to say, "I am a Christian. Can I pray for you?" She responded with enthusiasm, "Of course!" I prayed for peace in her life and relief from pain. When the prayer concluded, she turned to me and said firmly, "Now it is my turn. I will pray for you." Although her voice was weak and barely audible, her words carried immense power. She blessed me through her prayer, requesting, "Please grant Dr. Chae the strength and ability to continue caring for his patients, especially those suffering from diseases like mine." I was astounded by her radiant countenance, as I had just received a profound blessing from someone nearing the end of her life. This experience brought to mind the verse, "The one who was dying blessed me" (Job 29:13 NIV). It became evident that God was working mightily through our prayers, aiming to convey comfort and blessings to others. I felt deeply grateful.

These encounters illuminated how eagerly God awaits our prayers. I felt a sense of shame for the countless times I had promised to pray for someone but forgotten due to my busy life. Now, during rounds, I strive to pray on the spot when I feel the urge to do so. Sometimes, as I approach a patient's room, I find myself prepared to pray, and on emotionally charged days, I politely inquire whether I can pray for the patient. As we close our eyes in prayer, I imagine the joy it brings to God's heart.

Can I Pray for You?

Work through Prayer

I want to tell you a story of an Asian female cancer patient whom I was taking care of in Chicago. I remember she used to ask me a lot of questions about her illness and treatment. At the same time, she could not hide her anxiety in the face of impending death. She would tear up every time she mentioned her high school–aged daughter. All the medical staff in the ward liked her very much for her deep gratitude toward them.

Her disease progressed over time, and she had to be hospitalized frequently. I often found her looking restless. At one point during rounds, I asked her, "Is it okay if I pray for you?" Fortunately, she said yes. "God, please protect her heart and allow her to recover again, I earnestly pray to You," I said. After my prayer, she reported feeling better and thanked me.

At the next round, she told me an amazing story. Her daughter, who had been standing next to her listening to our prayer, had told her mother she also wanted to be a Christian. Then she called all her Christian friends at her school and asked them to pray for her mother. The patient added that she had bought a toy for her daughter when she was younger and that the hymn "Jesus Loves Me" came out when she pressed a button on the toy. And it occurred to me that one of the doctors in the lab told me he had a feeling during his prayers that the patient would meet God through her daughter.

I warned the patient that she might not have much time left if her body continued to weaken like this every day, despite my best efforts. I then asked her if she would be interested in hearing about my God. Thanks to her daughter, the patient opened up to God and answered that she would appreciate it. I told her about the God I love, the God who is pleased to give eternal life as a gift.

As she had been longing to meet her daughter again after her death, the patient accepted Jesus as her Lord, and her daughter did the same. God touched their souls through His love. The work of God's salvation was truly amazing. Although the patient soon passed away, I still keep in touch with her daughter. I have been sharing tips with her for college applications and wishing her the best.

Living a Life with Faith as Small as a Mustard Seed

Lastly, I want to tell the story of a young male cancer patient. He had been receiving targeted therapies and a series of radiation therapies because his cancer had spread to his brain. I invited him to a dinner after I gave a lecture at a local cultural center. Many people were praying for this patient. Every time I saw him, I sincerely wished he would befriend Jesus during his lonely and arduous journey with cancer.

At the end of his visit, I asked him if I could pray for him. I asked how he felt about God, then I shared the parable of the mustard seed. I explained the lesson, that is that we do not need incredible faith to believe in God; faith as small as a mustard seed, which has the potential to grow into a massive tree, or faith of only 0.1 percent, is enough for God to move mountains in our lives.

He said he would believe in God if "mustard seed faith" was all he needed. He expected God to fulfill the remaining 99.9 percent of his faith. Since he embarked on his spiritual journey, he has remained steadfast to God. We have become good friends.

It was purely God's work, as we had not planned any of this. I long for the Lord. I trust in Him and continue to look forward to seeing the grace of God at work in the hospital.

Every Moment Is God's Work

Speaking through Thoughts

One Sunday afternoon, I realized after I got home that I had forgotten to bring my laptop with me from the hospital. I was so exhausted from seeing so many patients that week that I felt too lazy to drive more than an hour to bring it back.

One patient suddenly came to mind; he was scheduled to undergo a surgical removal of his tumor. I was upset that he was all alone in his in-patient room due to COVID-19 visitor restrictions and could not spend time with his family before surgery. When my sadness did not lead to any further actions, God stepped in and asked me, *Would you like to be his family over the weekend?*

I decided to obey Him. Although I was not on-call, I rounded on all of my patients. When I entered that patient's room, my mentee first asked me to pray for her. I held her hand, and we prayed together for a long time. After spending more time with her, I took a picture with her and sent it to her family.

After rounding with me, my mentee asked me about my faith. Toward the end of our conversation, she accepted God as her Lord and Savior. Even during the pandemic, when everything came to a halt, God was still speaking to us through our thoughts and working through people who obey Him.

When I saw the patient again, I told him that the mentee who had come along with me the previous weekend had become a Christian. He was sincerely happy for my mentee; with a pure heart like a child, he took her hands and invited her into a prayer of celebration and blessings.

Working through the Situations

A lung cancer patient came to Chicago once every two months to receive medical treatment. He was a famous doctor in his country. Every time he came, an orthopedic surgeon at our hospital would come visit with him. I could tell that they were old friends. I was impressed by the surgeon's sincerity—he gave great attention to his friend's medical care and even called pharmaceutical companies to ensure that his friend received the correct medicine.

The patient initially responded well to targeted therapy; two years later, however, his condition took a turn for the worse, and he died of pneumonia. The surgeon contacted me afterward and thanked me for taking care of his friend. He told me to let him know if there was anything I needed in the future. I was really grateful, but I thought I would never need his help.

Ironically, I reached out to him very soon after that. One of my mentees, who was trained in orthopedics in Korea, was looking to build his career in the United States. When he got in touch with me, I had the idea of introducing him to that orthopedic surgeon. The surgeon generously offered to let my mentee participate in his clinic and the operating room. I was vaguely aware that my mentee had been praying earnestly to God while he was going through hard times; God, who works in every situation, answered his prayer by connecting me with the surgeon and the surgeon with my mentee.

I can now discern patterns in God's work. He helps someone in the most unexpected and sophisticated ways. Although I am familiar with the ways of God, I still look forward to what He has for each of us.

Keyword 7

Empathy: listen and listen with your heart

When I was in medical school, I was taught that doctors should always be unemotional and unbiased. I was also taught that doctors should not instill false hope in a patient; from a legal point of view, it is wise to explain every worst-case scenario from the very beginning. Furthermore, doctors are advised to distance themselves from patients in order to avoid emotional burnout.

My opinions have completely changed on this matter since I met Jesus. When I cry, Jesus cries with me. I dreamed of becoming a doctor who cries with his patients. The Bible teaches, "Rejoice with those who rejoice, and weep with those who weep" (Romans 12:15 KJV). The first reaction we have in the face of all sickness and suffering is lamentation. In the book of Psalms, more than a third of its content is about mourning.

In the United States, the term *lazarus response* refers to a situation in which a patient who was lying in bed like a dead body miraculously responds to treatment and is discharged from the hospital. This is an expression that derives its origin

Keyword 7

from the story of Jesus raising Lazarus from the dead. And this is the only time in the Bible when Jesus cries. The fact that Jesus identifies Himself with those He loves is consoling to me.

I once suggested hospice to a patient whose condition had deteriorated severely. The middle-aged female patient and her son immediately burst into tears. I felt a strong desire to pray for the patient. I knelt beside the bed, held the patient's hand, and asked if I could pray. While asking God to be with her and to give her peace, I could feel my throat aching. I finished my prayer with a trembling voice, as I was trying to hide my emotions.

I could hear my observing physician bawling from behind me. To be honest, I felt embarrassed. Nonetheless, when I looked at the patient, she had the brightest smile on her face. She said, "I am the happiest person in the world. I have two doctors who are crying for me."

I was not expecting her to say something like that. I realized then how powerful empathy can be, even at the end of life, and how important it is to deliver the heart of God to those who are in sorrow.

According to *Harvard Business Review*, the popular assumption that people who have been through a lot tend to be very empathetic can be wrong. They instead expect others to overcome hardships like they have and are disappointed when others fail.

Keyword 7

In the end, we need something extra in addition to our hardships in order to empathize with other people. That "something extra," I believe, comes from God, who is pouring out His heart to me. Empathy is not a skill, but rather an expression of sincerity. It is not about pretending to understand someone else's situation; it is simply about crying with that person. When I perform a physical exam on a patient, I will ask, "Is this tender?" The English word *tender* used in this context means "painful," but the word can also mean "soft." A heart that shares the pain is, in fact, a soft heart.

Albert's Tears

Paving the Way

God walks beyond the limits of my medical knowledge and takes a new path to heal patients. The story of my patient Albert Khoury's recovery through God's healing is something I still cherish to this day.

When I first saw Albert, he was in his early fifties, suffering from a rare lung cancer called mucinous adenocarcinoma. His cancer had already spread to both lungs. None of the treatments had worked for him. I placed him on several clinical trials, but the results were disappointing. His worsening symptoms finally led him to the intensive care unit (ICU).

Once stable, Albert showed an interest in lung transplantation. I explained that the medical literature excluded terminal cancer from the indications for transplant surgery. Albert insisted, claiming he had seen patients with terminal lung diseases enjoy a new life after receiving a lung transplant. He dreamed of being cancer-free at last. I spoke politely, saying, "Stage-four cancer cannot be treated with transplantation."

He said that no one had ever listened to his request. As I walked out of the ICU, I thought to myself, *In the case of Albert, the cancer cells have not yet spread elsewhere, other than his lungs. As long as we confirmed histologically that the thoracic lymph nodes were free of cancer, wouldn't it be possible to consider a transplant?*

I did not think I had the courage to act on my thoughts, however. The patient's condition was so bad, and I had never heard of any lung cancer cases that had been cured with a transplant. But as I walked out of the elevator and down the hospital corridor, I was surprised. I was shocked to see two thoracic surgeons, both experts in double-lung transplantation, having a discussion in that very hallway. I had never seen them together in that place. In fact, it felt like divine intervention. I interrupted their conversation and brought up my idea of performing a double-lung transplantation in my patient, Albert. What was even more surprising was that the two surgeons willingly agreed to proceed with the idea.

The surgeons asked me to present my patient at their transplantation conference. After an arduous approval process, Albert went through two months of extensive testing to ensure he was a good candidate for a double-lung transplantation. He surprisingly passed all the tests. He even recovered significantly after starting his new experimental targeted therapy, enabling him to continue pursuing diagnostic tests. The whole process went remarkably smoothly.

When he was only a step away from receiving the transplant, Albert developed pneumothorax and sepsis, requiring

ICU admission as well as intubation and vasopressors to stabilize him. He was in a critical situation in which he could pass away at any time. But on his third day in the ICU, a miracle happened. The surgical team received lungs from a brain-dead organ donor, and Albert was immediately transported, on his ventilator, into the operating room. The surgery was successful. I thanked God for this miracle. I later found out that Albert was able to receive the transplant more quickly than others on the transplantation list because of his clinical severity and admission to the ICU.

Since the surgery, Albert has been feeling well with his new lungs and has not experienced any relapse or transplant rejection. I think about God's guidance and protection every time Albert returns to the clinic for his three-month CT follow-up; he now has perfectly clear lungs, unlike most of my other patients. Even tests that detect circulating tumor DNA in the bloodstream continue to be negative, meaning that Albert has achieved the "cancer-free" state he so desired. His case is nothing short of a miracle.

For reference, these surgeries have previously been reported in similar cancers, but they have not become publicized for a number of reasons. The main reason is that stage-four lung cancer is usually considered a contraindication for transplantation. In Albert's case, the fact that his cancer was confined to both of his lungs without any distant spread allowed me to consider him for transplant surgery.

Now Albert is living a new life. As we have become good friends, he even agreed to speak at our testimony meeting.

He said he never gave up, knowing that he was receiving the best treatment possible. He told me that, as a Christian, he shouted the name of Jesus in his heart even when he was losing consciousness in the face of death in the ICU. When the evil spirits tried to take his life, he relied on Jesus until the end. He said he wanted to view each day as a gift from God and live his remaining days praying for others and encouraging them in their faith. While God gave him new life, His gift for me was meeting Albert.

God's Way Begins with Listening

The following is an email I received from a rehabilitation specialist who had been helping Albert adjust to his new challenges:

I've treated a lot of patients here, but it's my first time seeing a patient in tears while talking about his doctor. I've seen many patients resenting their doctors, but Albert was different; he kept crying as he told us about you, Dr. Chae. He said no one but Dr. Chae really listened to him and supported him. Even though I don't know you, I'm sending you this email because I want to tell you this story.

I was very emotional reading this email. I learned that God's way begins when we listen to another person. While I could have ignored Albert's request, I took the time to listen to him and see things in his perspective; afterward, God intervened and completed the rest of His work. As always, I was thankful to God for the plan He had shown to me.

Albert's Tears

Six months after the transplant, we hosted a party for Albert. Our work made it to the front page of the *Chicago Tribune* and appeared on several broadcasts around the world, including ABC and the BBC. For the first time, I was interviewed live on the U.S. radio station WGN. All of this felt like encouragement from God. My other patients also congratulated me in the clinic. One of them said, "I'm proud to have you as my doctor, Dr. Chae. I believe you are treating me with the same heart as you had for Albert." My patients' trust in me and gratitude for my work have been big sources of motivation for me. This entire process helped me experience God's presence in a more personal way.

I would like to summarize this special experience that God has given me with my poem called "Rehabilitation." Here are the last two lines: "I hear the sound of the heart beating again/ The sound of my injury healing/ The sound of the light coming in/ The sound of believing in God again/ The sound of welcoming love again/ I hear the sound of encouragement from heaven/ I know everything you have done/ You're doing so well/ You did a good job today/ I am proud of you."

You Are My Priority

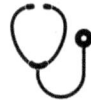

Rejoicing in Encouragement

Back when I was still in training, I did not fully understand how important it was to encourage and comfort my patients. More recently, while working in the clinic and observing God's work, I became interested in the physical and spiritual well-being of those for whom I was caring. It was only when I became a professor that I finally had a better awareness of how every word coming out of my mouth could affect a patient. Since I know my patients' diseases and treatments very well, patients expect me to understand them better than anyone else.

I learned that a small word of empathy can open a person's heart. I once heard about a surgeon who greeted his colorectal cancer patient in the following way: "How have you been? It must have been difficult living with an ostomy bag." Greeting a patient with words of empathy and compassion is a wonderful way to start the encounter. I frequently and intentionally ask the following of my patients: "You've been through so much. How are you feeling these days?"

You Are My Priority

I will never know unless I ask. "You are my priority" is what I want to convey. It is not my work as a physician, a research director, and an educator; my priority is the well-being of my patients. I often tell my patients, "I hope you endure the treatment well and see good results. I hope you recover. Your recovery is the most important thing to me."

These words have put many of my patients in tears. One patient even said my encouragement was her Christmas gift. I have been trying to use the word "hope" more frequently as I speak with my patients. Even in this age of defensive medicine, I still send the message that "I am on your side," "Your recovery is my source of happiness," and "I, as your doctor, wish for the same thing as you do."

There is no legal responsibility associated with the word "hope." While I still provide objective information about the natural course of the disease and the expected treatment results, my expression of hope at the end of the visit is separate from the prior discussion. I try to make it a habit to encourage my patients by speaking just a few additional words before ending the visit.

Some patients do not realize how resilient they have been throughout the course of treatment. Some do not know it is rare for anyone to respond for such a long period of time to a particular treatment. I try to tell my patients more often about how well they have been doing considering the severity of their diseases and the difficulty of treatment. I describe my emotions in words, too, so that my patients know I am happy for them. In difficult times, I tell them that I am moved by their perseverance.

As I said earlier, my team and I present awards to patients to congratulate them on meaningful milestones along their treatment journey. In particular, we encourage patients by creating various awards that are not related to the treatment results—such as the "best smile award," the "best couple award," and the "best fashion award." One of my mentees suggested that we give an award to a patient's wife, who had consistently been supportive to her husband. The wife became the first person to receive the "best caregiver award."

Neither patients nor guardians were expecting to receive an award from their health-care workers. When my co-workers and I encourage them through these award ceremonies, they appreciate the recognition, and a few people have even burst into tears. They admit that living with cancer or taking care of a cancer patient had been difficult, but the award gave them a source of motivation. These tears were tears of joy; no matter the treatment results, these tears were gifts of encouragement. Watching my patients delight in receiving awards like children receiving Christmas gifts, I reflected on the power of exchanging awards and encouraging each other.

Cheering for My Patients until the End

Having no more treatment options is every patient's worst nightmare. My patients occasionally ask me how many options they are left with. They fear that the fewer options, the sooner they will die. Fortunately, I work in an environment where I can think of many options through my expertise in clinical trials and my collaboration with free drug-supply programs by pharmaceutical companies, social work support programs at our hospital, and more. I am incredibly grateful for how much I can do for my patients. I rarely stop treating a patient due to a lack of options. I instead promise my patient I will somehow find the next best treatment every time. Regardless of the actual treatment results, the patients gather strength through this message of hope and support.

One of my patients was a young mother with two young children. The day after she passed away, her husband, Ryan, brought me a huge bouquet of flowers. I could not believe that he had thought of me so soon after his wife's death. He told me that she never lost any hope until the end; although she was aware of the severity of her disease, she continually pushed through each day, thanks to the messages of hope and encouragement she received from the medical staff. The husband wanted to show me his deep gratitude in this way. I realized that what is truly important in medicine is not a matter of life or death, but rather the attitude of a person facing death.

A common answer that my mentees gave when I asked them why they had decided to come to the United States was "to practice a better physician-patient relationship." Because doctor visits in Korea are typically less than fifteen minutes long, they thought it would be difficult to build a strong rapport with their patients there. I also have acquaintances who were hurt by arrogant, overbearing doctors and were searching for doctors with whom they would feel more comfortable.

Even here in the United States, when patients do not like their doctors' attitude, they often go "doctor shopping" to find a new one. Patients sometimes experience more difficulty from misunderstandings and conflicts arising from the doctor-patient relationship than solely from their physical pain. There are times when patients continue to receive treatment despite feeling burdened by their relationship with doctors. It hurts me every time I hear these stories.

I believe God has called us not to have work, but to have relationships. A relationship that gives you rest can become your source of recovery. You do not rest in order to work; rest is a purpose in itself. How good would it be if patients could feel relaxed and accepted, and gain strength through their relationships with doctors? I hope that every doctor's visit is used as an opportunity to cultivate a beautiful relationship with a patient. I wish that the clinic becomes a place where treatment results do not affect the trust in doctor-patient relationship, where the relationship resembles that of a marathon runner and a pacemaker, or a pacesetter.

I have an Asian patient who usually comes to her visit accompanied by her middle-aged daughter; the daughter helps the mother communicate her concerns in English. I enjoy seeing them smile like innocent children. I gave them a thumbs-up once for smiling so much and being so adherent to treatment. The daughter also told me that her father's face brightens whenever my name is brought up in the conversation; he is always looking for me every time his wife is hospitalized. I like him very much as well.

I often prayed that I would like to love my patients more; God has been answering this prayer. The Asian patient told me she looks forward to every visit because she misses me. How wonderful would it be if all my patients thought of me as a good friend whom they could not wait to see again. As a good friend would do, I send sympathy cards to the families after the loss of their loved ones to express my heartfelt condolences and unwavering support. A message that I like to write in these cards is this:

The times I spent with your loved one in the clinic left behind good memories, and I miss those moments. It was an honor to be able to take care of the patient.

Rounds Include Family, Too

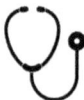

He Told Me to Take Care of the Patient's Family

At some point, I started to feel more sympathy toward the caregivers. They seemed emotionally drained and physically exhausted. I wanted to do anything I could to comfort and encourage them.

One married couple from Greece taught me to love caregivers. I had been treating the wife for a while, and she had finally begun to recover after her chemotherapy treatments, when suddenly the husband was diagnosed with terminal cancer. He became my patient, as well. I remember crying while praying for this couple. The wife was especially very worried, so we often prayed holding our hands together.

I once asked the husband, before he became my patient himself, how he was doing. He looked into my eyes for a moment, then grabbed my hand and cried. His cries turned into sobs. No one had likely asked him that question before. I also tried my best to check in on their three children, who suddenly had two parents with cancer and needed their

Rounds Include Family, Too

attention. I thanked the children for taking care of their sick parents so diligently.

Shortly after the wife passed away, the husband followed. Amazingly, although the husband showed the medical signs of approaching death, he stayed alive for a few more weeks while his three children came to spend time with him. The children later told me, "Doctor, I think our father wanted to see the three of us together. We've been so busy for a while that we couldn't be together like this on a daily basis. I think seeing us get along for the past couple weeks made him happy."

They reminded me of the Bible verse found in Psalm 133:1: "How good and how pleasant it is when brothers truly live together in unity!" (NET).

I thought it might please God if I were to call on deceased patients' family members to check in and see how they were doing. I started "making my rounds" to family members by calling the patient's spouse, parents, and/or children. Before calling them, I would pray, *God, I hope they feel Your consolation.* To be honest, I was not sure what to say to those who were grieving. I just started by saying that I had called to hear their voice, that I was wondering if they were doing well, and that I, too, missed the patient.

One husband told me through tears that he had learned to take walks when the sadness was too difficult to bear. A wife shared her memories of her beloved husband—how he was the best husband, the best father, the best neighbor, and overall an amazing gift from God. She added that her husband had loved his disabled son dearly and was sad he could not be there for the son; she hoped they would meet again in heaven. I was so grateful to hear these stories, and I also wept as I heard her words. Another husband said it was a great blessing to have spent a lot of time with his wife, so much that he could not even pray to God to give them more time. Although she had died, he wept with gratitude that they had met such great medical staff and had received good treatment, regardless of the outcome. One patient's daughter answered my phone call so happy and excited, asking if I had really called to hear her voice. Through these "family rounds," God had me shed His tears.

No one knows the pain and suffering of patients better than their caregivers and their doctor. Similarly, no one knows how consistently the guardians cared for the patients in the hospital better than the medical staff. It is, therefore, a great source of strength for caregivers when the medical staff expresses appreciation for their hard work.

I wish I had known earlier that my words of encouragement could mean so much to my patients and their caregivers. I regretted that I had missed out on so many opportunities due to my self-centeredness, my introversion, and my busy schedule. From now on, I have vowed to pour out God's love to my patients and their families.

The amazing thing is that God, through having me make family rounds, has also touched my heart. He had me rethink the meaning of life and helped me discover my mission of comforting and encouraging others. When the caregivers ask

Rounds Include Family, Too

me to do more research so their loved ones' deaths are not in vain, I find a holy motivation to work harder. The process of using the knowledge and wisdom gained from having treated my deceased patients and applying those lessons to the treatment of new patients is very rewarding. The husband of Judy, one of my patients who passed away from lung cancer, sent me this letter:

> Dear Professor Chae and the medical team,
>
> How are you doing? I am writing this letter to thank you for the special and compassionate care my wife received from you while battling small cell lung cancer.
>
> From our first day of treatment in 2019 to the last day of treatment in 2020, we clearly knew that we were receiving the highest level of treatment in the world. We were tremendously impressed with your ability to clarify all situations and the sincerity in your thorough explanations regarding what exactly was happening right now and what could also happen in the future. I never once felt like the treatment was rushed or careless. You guys always listened to all of our requests and answered all of our questions. We knew Judy was getting the best care that U.S. medicine could offer.
>
> Every time we left the 17th floor of the Galter Building [the building where the oncology clinic was located], we felt encouraged and hopeful. Even when dealing with a diagnosis that wasn't easy to accept, thanks to your support, we had room to hope that good things could happen. Judy wanted to beat the disease and vowed to contribute to Professor Chae winning the Nobel Prize. We even discussed what we would wear to the Nobel Prize award ceremony in Stockholm.

One suggestion I have is that when a patient receives chemotherapy in the Arkes building, I wish a family member could accompany the patient. The room seemed to have enough space for the doctors to administer chemo even while socially distancing themselves from the caregivers. Luckily, I was able to be with Judy via video calls, but it would have been so much better if we had been physically together. The process of receiving chemotherapy is not only confusing and scary, but also an arduous and tiring process that's difficult to experience alone.

Thank you for everything you did for my wife.

Regards, L

We were so thankful the husband pointed out the strict visitor restriction policy implemented during the COVID-19 pandemic and suggested ways in which we can improve. These letters I receive from families after their loss contribute greatly to my conviction that research is one way to love my patients and their caregivers and believe that the patient was and is still loved by their family. Some family members have even donated to our medical school to support my research. I came to a new realization that my research could be a source of consolation for the family members.

An Unforgettable Funeral

Once, a deceased patient's son and wife visited my office. They were a Black family living in South Chicago. They came to my office to personally invite me and my medical staff to the patient's funeral. At first, I refused, with the excuse that I

Rounds Include Family, Too

was too busy, but after seeing their deep sorrow and sincere request, I decided to attend.

Three members of the medical staff and I attended the Saturday morning funeral. I was very touched by the service. It took place in a very large, beautiful Black church. The choir sang "Oh, Happy Day" and prayed for the patient to go to heaven. Many people came forward and shared their memories and the grateful times they had with the patient. Hearing these stories made me think, *Oh, he was someone with such a beautiful personality.* The wife also gestured to me, and I went up to the pulpit with my team members to share a few words:

"It is a great honor to be here to support and comfort Mr. B's family members while commemorating his life alongside his relatives. I am an oncologist at the cancer center of Northwestern University. I treat many kinds of cancers, including the lung cancer that Mr. B had. Three members of my medical team—Reena, Ally, and Linda—are also here to join you. I'm so happy and grateful that we can be here with you.

We have received a lot of funeral invitations in the past, but this was the first time the family had visited us personally, sincerely thanked us for our kindness, and invited us to the funeral. I still cannot forget the tears the wife and son shed that day. I could feel the family's deep affection and pride for Mr. B, and I could sense the sincerity in how they honored the deceased together. We were with Mr. B during his final months as he fought the deadly cancer. He had such a beautiful personality. He was very kind, and we were happy every time he visited our clinic. He endured the treatment so well, but death suddenly came to him. We were all in the midst of sadness.

Lung cancer still ranks first in mortality among all cancers to this day. Approximately 160,000 people die due to lung cancer in the United States each year. Unfortunately, lung cancer is often only detected in the later stages, after the cancer has already progressed significantly. Good treatments are being developed, but we still have a long way to go to cure the disease. My research team and I, as well as many other teams in the United States, are conducting much research to save the lives of others like Mr. B.

I want to congratulate Mr. B. I believe that he was not a victim of lung cancer; rather, he was a victor who fulfilled the many missions of life that God had prepared for him. One of those missions was getting through life as a cancer patient. When I reflect on how well he and his family endured this difficult task, I think about how beautiful and reliable they were in their faith in God.

We often see families blaming each other in these situations, but this family was the exact opposite. They were always there for each other. It was truly a rare sight. As we celebrate Mr. B's life and his return home, to heaven, we are reminded that death is not the end, but the beginning of a new life. I bless you all in the name of God."

I would like to introduce a poem I wrote with a promise to meet my patient again in heaven.

Blue

by
Young Kwang Chae

Some say that COVID-19 blues don't exist in a hospital
But when I exchange looks of despair and hope with patients
With spit particles splashing my mask as I explain,
My soul is breathless

Occasionally, I close my eyes out of fatigue without even realizing
And a blue wave approaches me from my desk
The fresh beach sand tickles my toes
Wow, the dazzling white island of Santorini spreads out in front of me
The legendary island that was hardened by lava that passed by the beautiful Aegean Sea

So now, I toss my fatigue into Santorini and rub my eyes to wake up
To meet my patient who went to hospice yesterday
I put on a new white coat
When I look down, I realize my scrubs are Santorini blue
Smelling the saltiness of the sea, I walk to the Aegean, where my patient is waiting

After the patient graduated from hospice
We promised to meet each other again as if nothing had happened

On the blue sea
The white island
The blue church
In front of the white stairs

Keyword 8

Best: one who is more sincere than I

Many people work very hard behind the scenes to ensure that patients receive the best treatment. Although I try to spend as much time as possible with patients in the clinic, it feels very short compared to the time my co-workers and I put into preparing for treatment.

Before I see a patient in the clinic, I look at all the diagnostic images and compare them to the previous results. All the blood tests on that day are compared to the previous data, and I graph the differences. I carefully review each marker in the tissue biopsies. If I see the need to change the treatment, I look for a clinical trial that is appropriate to the patient's phase and consult with clinical trial researchers. If I want to use a drug that is not being studied in a clinical trial, then I find out whether that drug can be covered by the patient's insurance. If the drug is not approved or is too expensive, I communicate with the social workers to see if there are any hospital or group funds that can help the patient. If I want to use a drug that has not yet been approved by the Food and Drug Administration (FDA) for the patient's specific condition, I contact the pharmaceutical company directly to apply

Keyword 8

for a program that provides the drug for free. If I think that radiation therapy or surgery will be necessary in the middle of the treatment process, doctors from various specialties will gather to examine the patient's situation and prepare a meeting to think about the best treatment plan together. If I have a question, I seek real-time advice from colleagues.

I create educational materials for patients who are starting new treatment scenes to ensure that patients receive the regimens. I prepare a consent form for patients on clinical trials. If the patient does not speak English, I not only write a translated version in advance, but I also arrange for a translator to be present during the patient visit. For patients with transportation issues, I connect them to a taxi service sponsored by the American Cancer Association. Finally, I prepare for Plan B for any unexpected turn of events. As such, I spend much more time outside the patient's room than I do with patients one-on-one in the clinic.

Then I came to the realization that God had been faithfully working day and night behind the scenes for me. Even when I am not actively praying and worshiping Him, God was still attentive, and He understood me inside and out. I had chances to listen to God's words and testimonies on similar topics, and I felt that it was God's hand specifically guiding me toward the right path.

God's provision always goes above and beyond my best hopes and expectations. As I witness firsthand how all things come together for His glory, I am able to truly trust and rely on the verse: "Surely goodness and mercy shall follow me all

Keyword 8

the days of my life; and I will dwell in the house of the Lord Forever" (Psalm 23:6 NKJV).

After witnessing miraculous treatment responses and watching our co-workers try their best to help patients until their very last moments, some of my fellows decided to accept God. We have learned that God has been working ahead of us in ways big and small. He guided us to get a drug approved by an insurance or pharmaceutical company despite our initial rejection, He helped us launch a clinical trial right when my patient needed one, and He helped us gain approval for a patient assistance fund that seemed unlikely to be approved. I praise and thank God for all the great and unsearchable things He has shown us through this process.

Research Begins with Love for Patients

Sending Love through Research

"What wakes you up every morning?"

This question appeals to me a lot. One of the many things that motivates me to wake up every morning is my passion for research. As I spend my time in the clinic/hospital setting—a very organized society—there are times when I feel the center of my attention shifts from caring for patients to receiving honor and recognition from other people. This desire is particularly strong among doctors working at large university hospitals, as we are evaluated by the grade and number of our published papers, which is the key determining factor of promotions. This is just our reality.

When I was working as a researcher at Johns Hopkins Hospital, I was afraid that my experiments might fail; in that case, not only would I not be able to write a good thesis, but I was also worried about authorship when I was involved in a group project. The time I spent working in this lab was daunting and stressful; I felt alone and unsupported.

After God began to give me feelings of compassion toward my patients, I sincerely hoped my research would improve their lives. I no longer cared whether or not I was the first author. Instead, I longed to share my research ideas and passion with others, and I did not mind if others became the first author using my ideas—I was content as long the published research could help extend the lives of cancer patients. I was even grateful when someone with more ability, time, and stamina than me performed the research using my ideas.

The thought that I could love my patients through research was inspiring. However, pharmaceutical companies have a different motivation; the purpose of a business is to make a profit. Therefore, pharmaceutical companies work to develop only marketable drugs. On the other hand, doctors can do research for their patients even if their patients cannot afford medical treatment. No matter how expensive a drug is, if it is effective in treating cancer, clinical research can be conducted with support from the government or a nonprofit organization. Research on the development of rare cancer treatments does not receive much financial support nor interest from pharmaceutical companies. But if data on these rare cancer treatments accumulate over time, I believe that one day we will be able to treat that rare cancer. These days, one in four diagnosed cases of cancer are rare cancers.

With this mindset, I decided to gather all the data from my rare cancer patients, and I envisioned, designed, and conducted a new trial called DART (Dual Anti-CTLA-4 and Anti-PD-1 Blockade in Rare Tumors) through the largest clinical trial group called SWOG, where I serve as the co-chair. DART is an innovative clinical trial that classifies rare cancer into fifty-five different groups and treats them in a single trial. The drug of interest simultaneously inhibits CTLA4 and PD-1, which are drug targets discovered by the joint winners of the 2018 Nobel Prize in Physiology, Professor Jim Alison and Professor Tasuku Honjo, respectively. So far, about eight hundred patients have participated in the past four years. The trial is being conducted at more than one thousand hospitals across the United States. In addition to my role as the co-chair, I worked as the general manager of all the studies that made use of the patients' blood and tissue samples.

When I hear stories of patients whose cancers have not grown as a result of the DART trial, the joy I feel is immense. A news reporter once visited my lab to investigate the story of a twenty-seven-year-old male cancer patient who had a refractory adenocarcinoma of the adrenal cortex that was now responding well to the investigation drug. When the DART trial became publicized, I became even more enthusiastic about conducting this research to help save patients. The American Academy of Cancer Research (AACR) journals selected the DART trial as the most cited research. It was even included in the NCCN guidelines for the U.S. standard for chemotherapy.

Research Is Another Way of Loving Patients

When you spend a lot of time in the lab, you encounter many people—people who are there to add another line to their résumés; residents and fellows who are there in hopes of boosting their applications; people who are there to just keep their place as a "researcher"; people who are there to just receive funding. There is nothing as sad as watching research that started out of passion turn into just a load of work. As someone who has also gone through these struggles, I constantly talk to my mentees about using research as a way to truly love their patients instead of just a shortcut to success.

I want my mentees to learn not from the perspective of pharmaceutical companies and hospital managers, but from that of the patients. One of my favorite things to hear from my mentees is that they are happy to have finally realized that research is a way to love their patients. One should never start a clinical trial that lacks scientific evidence or is ethically problematic. I sincerely want my patients to have good results through the clinical trials I recommend, so I tell them, "My goals for this clinical research are the same as yours—I want the best outcome. But I cannot promise any results. However, there is one thing that I can guarantee: I am going to put you first. Nothing comes before you—not the clinical trial, not the pharmaceutical companies, not the hospital administration that sponsors this research. You, my patient, come first."

Research Begins with Love for Patients

Like many of my colleagues, I had the experience of leading a clinical trial for a single patient. I even wrote the protocols for a clinical trial and went through every step of the complicated administrative process to get a drug approved. In addition, I planned and conducted a great deal of translational research to derive meaning from patients' tissue and blood samples. It is essential to conduct proper translational research during a clinical trial. We must be reminded that patients are risking their lives by deciding to participate in clinical trials. The only way to understand why they are not responding to certain drugs is through translational research. We should not miss this one and only opportunity provided by the patient to study their blood and tissue samples; therefore, each study must be preceded by good planning and determination of which biomarkers to use as clues. It is a pleasure and honor to present a research plan, conduct research, and suggest better treatments through my work.

I want to cure patients, but at the same time, I feel very sad when I see them suffer from the side effects of treatment. I often see my patients living longer with immunotherapy. However, in a few rare cases, immunotherapy can actually increase the growth of cancerous cells (a process called hyperprogression), resulting in relapsed cancer. One of the ongoing studies in my lab concerns defining hyperprogression and determining its causes. I always try to keep myself in check any time I feel I may know everything there is to know about these drugs. We still do not exactly understand why a drug that works on some patients does not work on others and why a drug causes side effects on some but not others.

When I am serving the sick, my service can actually become poisonous if I do not let go of the pride that comes with thinking I absolutely know what is best for them. As a result, I am constantly studying with a humble mind and a loving heart for my patients.

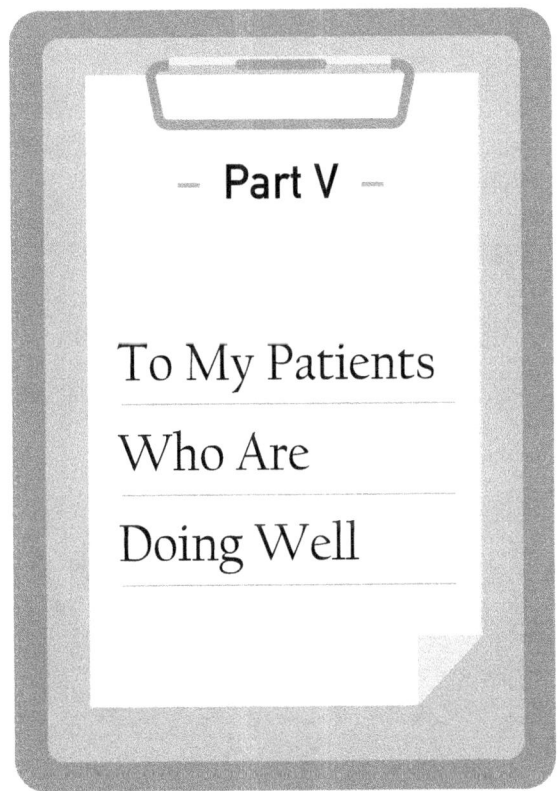

Part V

To My Patients Who Are Doing Well

May I Come In?

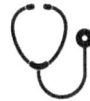

Treating Patients as Friends

Love is about asking questions. Unlike what takes place in the Korean clinic system, patients in the United States enter an examination room first, and then I go into the rooms to see them. Before I enter any of the rooms in which a patient is waiting, I always ask first, "May I come in?" Even if I knock, I know it is rude to open the door and enter right away. I should only do things as far as my patients allow. Whether it is sharing bad news, such as a cancer diagnosis, or discussing various treatment methods, it is wise to first ask how much they want to know—how prepared they are to have a discussion and how well they already know about their situation. As I knock on the doors to the patients' rooms, I often imagine myself asking if I can enter their lives and start treating their diseases. We often talk about *evidence-based medicine,* but we sometimes forget about *etiquette-based medicine.*

It is important for doctors to be at the same eye level as the patient—bringing in a chair to sit, and when there is no extra chair in the room, even kneeling to see eye to eye; placing a hand on the patient's shoulder or arm to let them know that I am with them in the moment; directing my eyes and body toward the patient, etc. I try to communicate nonverbally to convey the message that they are the most important thing to me in that moment.

Sometimes my patients apologize for talking too much and taking up my time. The more I hear their apologies, though, the more I try to make them feel like they are my priority. For patients who have had to wait a long time, I sincerely apologize.

When I treat patients with this mindset of putting them first, I discover a friend in me. I ask if their family is doing well and sometimes go further to specifically ask where they went on vacation. Some patients even wish me happiness. Even though they are going through the most difficult times of their lives, they check up on me when they notice my fatigue.

I miss the patients who have passed away; we were friends. Instead of being remorseful, however, I imagine them happily living in heaven with their new, healthy bodies.

Realizing That Medicine Is Not Only a Skill

I feel proud when my mentees learn through observing my work that medicine is not only about skills, but also about the art of relationships. I would like to share two of my mentees' testimonials.

May I Come In?

First, Hyung-Kyu Cho testified:

"I've experienced something amazing today. While observing Dr. Chae's clinic, I asked myself for the first time, *I wonder how the patients feel.*

One old lady, who was regressing to childlike behavior, was losing her vision and could no longer read books. A young cancer patient in her thirties with abnormal test results asked me with a sullen face what the results meant. A patient in her forties asked questions and meticulously took notes about her clinical trial. The list goes on. Today, I have finally begun to 'see' these patients; I could see each patient as a living person with his or her own life.

Before, I would have complained about why these patients have so many questions; but today, I was not my old self. I was able to see how worried they must be, how scared they must be, and how sad they must be.

One thing that's for certain is that I alone am definitely not capable of this level of empathy. If the Holy Spirit did not give me the heart to empathize, I would not be able to understand their affliction and love my neighbors. Today, I received a hint from God about what mindset I should have as a doctor and what kind of doctor I want to be. Today's experience enlightened me on patient perspectives. It was truly precious and priceless. I would like to pray every day to be able to love my patients."

My other mentee, Grace Lee, who has dreamed of being a doctor since she was a child and has worked hard to achieve this dream, was shocked when she heard the news of her own grandmother's terminal cancer. Seeing her debilitated,

Can I Pray for You?

bedridden grandmother rendered her speechless. She felt uneasy when her grandmother tried to comfort her.

After the loss of her beloved grandmother, Grace was left only with regrets. Around that time, she joined my lab. She testified:

> "When I first joined the lab, I had to work from home through Zoom meetings for the first few months due to the pandemic. Only when the new quarter started in September was I able to enter the clinic with Dr. Chae.
>
> I saw a lot of cancer patients with Dr. Chae every week. I met a lot of people—from those who were the same age as me to those who were around the same age as my grandmother. I carefully observed how Dr. Chae was treating the patients—how he talked to patients, how he respected the patients, and how he encouraged the patients.
>
> The professor often told the patients, 'I'm glad you are doing well.' Patients rejoiced when they heard this. I think they felt comforted by the reassurance that they were doing well and relieved that the doctor was happy for them. The professor also emphasized often that the patients, medical staff, and caregivers are all on the same team. When the patients were told that everyone was doing their best and hoping for their recovery, they felt reassured; for them, it was like having a thousand soldiers standing behind them in support. The professor spent a lot of time with each patient, listening to their stories to the end.
>
> If I could meet my grandmother again, I would like to tell her warm words of comfort with my renewed heart. But because I know it is impossible to meet her again in this world, I want to comfort other patients and give them the best care possible with the same mindset as this."

It's Not Your Fault

It is nobody's fault.

Many times, patients want to find the specific cause of their disease. They often wonder if they did anything wrong. Furthermore, they suffer from guilt. I have also seen patients and caregivers believing discouraging myths.

Their fears gave me the idea to offer a seminar called "Everything You Need to Know about Cancer" to patients and caregivers at nearby cancer support groups, health promotion centers, Korean cultural centers, churches, and cathedrals. I was never asked to give a talk, but I actively contacted patients and caregivers, telling them I would give them a free lecture on this topic. There is one thing I emphasize in these lectures: terminal diseases are *not* the patient's fault, nor is it *anyone's* fault. Of course, risk factors exist, but the existence of a risk factor does not guarantee a diagnosis. Chronic smoker Winston Churchill never got lung cancer, but his late brother-in-law, who had never smoked a cigarette in his life, died of lung cancer. This is because approximately 15 percent of lung cancers occur in non-smokers. In my first encounter with patients, I try to emphasize that the cancer is not their fault. In fact, the most powerful risk factor for cancer is age. Genetic replication occurs every time a cell divides, and as you get older, the number of times your cells replicate increases, hence resulting in a greater chance that such abnormalities will occur at random. Anomalies in the genes are the most common root cause of cancer.

In some cases, patients search for a scapegoat. One mother lamented that her daughter got cancer because her husband and mother-in-law did not take care of her. One male patient with a family history of cancer blamed his parents. Already drained both physically and mentally, patients can have a breakdown if the blame game continues.

In other cases, patients blame God. One patient had devoted her entire life to her dry-cleaning business to make money to care for their children. Just as she was planning a vacation to finally enjoy her life, she was diagnosed with terminal cancer. People often say God is too cruel. But if you enter this blame game, you will feel very depressed and fall into a cycle of shutting yourself away from your loved ones—and God—who are the ones who can help you the most. Therefore, the diagnosis of a serious disease such as cancer often leads to many spiritual problems, on top of the already-existing physical pain.

God Weeps with Us

Sickness is not a curse. God is never pleased when we suffer. He is not one to think, *Ah, how satisfying!* and secretly laugh about our pain. Suffering was never God's intention. Jeremiah 33:3 (NIV) says, "Call to me and I will answer you and tell you great and unsearchable things you do not know." The original heart of God is also found in Ezekiel 18:32 (ESV): "Have I any pleasure in the death of the wicked, declares the Lord God, and not rather that he should turn from his way and live?" God wants us to turn to Him even in our most painful moments. Sickness is not God's way of punishing or cursing us. Even in our pain and suffering, God is suffering with us. Jesus is Someone who cries even with those in the lowest, most painful places.

One of the performers on America's long-running show *America's Got Talent* was a singer from Ohio called Nightbirde. She had cancer all over her body when she appeared on the show. And yet she sang a self-composed song titled "It's Okay," and she got the Golden Buzzer, taking her straight to the semifinals. She told the judges, "I want people to know that I am much more than the unfortunate thing that happened to me." The audience was impressed by her bright aura and comforting song. On her blog, she wrote about how it felt when she was wrestling with God during her cancer treatments. She suffered from the side effects of chemotherapy, resulting in intense bowel pain; she sometimes even fell asleep on the toilet.

"The reason why some people can't see God is that they don't know how to look lower. That's right—you have to seek from a lower place. My God is on the bathroom floor."

Miracles Begin Once You Let Go of Numbers

Freeing Oneself from the Confines of Statistics Leads to a Miracle

I often check to see whether my patients are fixated on statistics during treatment. In movies and shows, and sometimes even in reality, doctors say things, such as "You have six months left," which may sound like a death sentence to most patients. It is an unfortunate sight to see. I never talk about numbers when patients ask me how much time they have left.

One of my patients was responding well to her chemotherapy. When she heard from another department about her expected life expectancy, however, she suddenly began to suffer from insomnia. Based on clinical data, we can often estimate the numbers. However, estimating is not the same as predicting. It is outside of our realm to accurately predict how much time patients have left and personalize it based on their exact situation. Only God knows how much time any of us have left. I only provide a general time frame—around a

Miracles Begin Once You Let Go of Numbers

few days/weeks/months/years—and never anything specific. The moment I say a number out loud, though, patients can get tied down to it and start counting down to the end of their lives.

I tell my patients to prepare mentally and economically for the risk of sudden complications, such as pneumonia or thrombosis, which can result from cancer and may lead to death. But I sincerely hope that none of my patients take their cancer diagnosis as a death sentence and feel crushed by sorrow and despair, counting down to their "day of execution." Even if I do not mention any statistics, however, many patients search up online and come to me in a state of shock. I always tell these patients resolutely, "These average statistics are not *your* statistics. These statistics include outliers, such as people who died right after their diagnosis, as well as people who died several years after. They have nothing to do with you." I think accepting this is very important for patients to allow space for God to work.

Patients also want to hear the word *cure*. When I'm explaining the details regarding the disease and the prognoses of their cancer, they often ask if it's possible to get cured in the middle of treatment. If the cancer has progressed throughout the body, the probability of getting completely cured is very low. Nonetheless, I never use words like *absolutely* or *impossible*.

Medicine is the study of probability. It is not like math, where there is always an exact answer. Medicine always contains room for uncertainty. In my experience in the

Can I Pray for You?

clinic, I have often seen things occur that are not explained in textbooks. I have seen so-called miracles occur in medicine. Sometimes when I discontinue chemotherapy due to a patient's report of severe fatigue, the cancer stops progressing at the same time, and the patient is suddenly able to continue on with life like nothing had ever happened. I am sure many other doctors have seen unexplainable cases like these. That is why I never use the word *incurable* when talking with patients. Instead, I describe cancer as a "difficult situation." I tell them their cancer is treatable and that therapy can be used to prolong their lives. Patients regain happiness even when hearing that treatment is possible.

Some patients express difficulty continuing with treatment after their doctors tell them exactly how much time is left. It is difficult for doctors to tell patients to wait for a miracle.

When I was in Houston, one of my church friends became my patient. She had previously heard she only had five years left to live, but here she was in the clinic on her seventeenth year of chemotherapy, treating the cancer that had spread all over her body. Her telling me that she went jogging every morning, nonetheless, was very memorable to me. I heard that she lived for five more years even after I had left Houston. Thankfully, I have many patients, who have been told to consider hospice, find my clinic and achieve stable disease for several years.

I also believe in the therapeutic effects of intercessory prayer. I believe that God performs miracles to cure diseases.

Miracles Begin Once You Let Go of Numbers

To be completely honest, as a doctor, I confess that it is sometimes difficult to maintain faith knowing how difficult it is statistically to treat cancer. But since our lives are under God's sovereignty, I believe that God will be very pleased to see that we pray for healing and recovery to the very end. David also prayed earnestly for his sick wife and children to be able to live. While it is in the realm of God to heal or not heal the sick, I at least do not want to get in the way of God's miracle due to my lack of faith.

I Want to Complain to the Lord for My Patients

Jesus miraculously cured a patient with hemophilia and told him that it was his faith that had saved him. This is why a patient's faith is so important. But in the case of the four friends who broke through the roof and brought a paralyzed man to Jesus, Jesus saw *their* faith and performed a miracle.

I want to be a friend like this to my patients. I want to be a friend who can bring my patients to Jesus and pray for a miracle to occur. Even when Jesus healed a woman's daughter, He praised her faith and said that everything would unfold as much as they prayed and wished for it. The woman surrendered her pride and begged Jesus for her daughter's survival. I want to do the same for my patients. I want to create a space for the Lord to work despite the voice in the back of my head reminding me of a patient's statistical prognosis. Instead I humbly pray to Jesus, *If You are able, please heal them,* and

Jesus responds, "If thou canst believe, all things are possible to him that believeth" (Mark 9:23 KJV).

There is another element of truth to the story of the paralytic. While it was the four friends who pleaded for their friend's physical recovery, Jesus first proclaimed, "Take heart, son; your sins are forgiven" (Matthew 9:2 NIV). After forgiving the friends, He then healed the paralyzed man. Here, we see that God wants us to live eternally through repentance of our sin instead of through this physical body that will one day erode and become corrupt. As I pray for my patients, I look up to Jesus, who saves us both physically and spiritually. Under His guidance, I turn my clinic into a mission field.

Keyword 9

Acceptance: there is no miracle on the cross

I love the saying, "There is no miracle on the cross." Even Jesus could not come down from the cross. At times, no matter how much we pray, a situation takes a turn for the worse. In these situations, there are no words more comforting than "There is no miracle on the cross." To believe in Jesus is to suffer with Him or to fulfill the rest of His sufferings. When we walk on the path toward the cross, the path of suffering, we may not experience any miracles. We must look to Jesus, who has walked along this same path before us.

Many times, we think of a disease as a trial. It is said that we are given two rewards after overcoming the trial: the crown of the world and the crown of heaven. Daniel prayed earnestly only to fall into the lions' cave, and Mordecai praised only God but was sentenced to death. Joseph, after overcoming the trial of the flesh, was sent to prison, and Job sincerely respected God, only for his entire family to be destroyed, his business to go bankrupt, and for him to suffer from a terrible skin disease. But after each of these obstacles was over, God

Keyword 9

rewarded all the injustices and exalted them above all else. This is the crown of the world.

On the other hand, Peter and Paul preached diligently but were stoned and eventually killed. While Peter led the disciples by preaching to three thousand people at once, John lived quietly with Jesus' mother and was exiled, dying on an island. John the Baptist was beheaded despite the earnest prayers of his disciples, and Jonathan, David's loyal friend, died miserably on the battlefield. From the perspective of the world, their deaths would have raised doubts regarding the existence of God. However, they died because they did not receive the crown of the world, but instead they received the crown of heaven.

We must remember the fact that Jesus Himself accepted His death on the cross. It was God's providence to hold and accept the suffering as it was instead of avoiding it. The reason miracles do not exist on the cross is that it is the Lord's will to carry the burdens of the cross.

At one point, I thought the reason for our sufferings was to be used by God for a greater cause in the future. Now I know I was wrong. God might not use our sufferings in any way at all. Isn't enduring these challenges a reward in itself?

I would be grateful for receiving the crown of the world, and I would equally be grateful for receiving the crown of heaven in the future. I want to give the Lord a prayer of gratitude regardless of the result. I believe He wants me to grow into a more mature person through enduring the difficulties

Keyword 9

and injustices that occur in the hospital. During my struggle, I remember the words of the Lord telling us to follow Him to the cross.

God does not actually need me. God created the heavens and the earth without me, and He can send down angels and make everyone believe in Him without my help. He is just giving me the opportunity to build my own blessings. I believe that "anyone who wants to come to him must believe that God exists and that he rewards those who sincerely seek him" (Hebrews 11:6 NLT), and that God prepares our rewards as abundantly as our hard work has been.

Together through Mourning and Hope

Crying with the Pandemic

In the spring of 2020, COVID-19 hit Chicago. Both patients and staff members in our cancer center died from complications due to the virus. It was an emergency situation in which even the fellows had to work full-time on the COVID-19 unit. In this unprecedented time, I began to ask God how I should comprehend this situation.

How should we understand the coronavirus pandemic in the light of our faith? Was the pandemic also part of "God's will"? Perhaps a wise question is more important than a wise answer. Before I tried to interpret the situation, I wanted to first learn about what the Bible says about diseases and human suffering. I often ask "why" God allows certain people to have certain diseases. God may allow suffering and disease, but He does not intentionally cause them. The Bible says that God does not take pleasure in our suffering.

As Romans 8:22 says, we can try to understand sickness from the perspective that "all creation has been groaning as in the pains of childbirth" (NLT). In that sense, sickness is the groan of all humans and creatures, and it signals the expectation of a new heaven, a new earth, and a new body in the resurrection. People asked Jesus about a man who was blind from birth, whether the reason for his blindness was his own sins or the sins of his parents. I have been wanting to ask the same question. At that time, Jesus answered, "It was not that this man sinned, or his parents, but that the works of God might be displayed in him" (John 9:3 ESV).

Sickness is not the result of sin. Jesus proved the glory of God by healing the blind man, demonstrating a "future-oriented" understanding of disease, not a "past-oriented" one. If we are currently suffering from a specific disease for reasons we do not fully understand, it means that when we depend on the Lord, the glory of God can be revealed through us.

It can, indeed, be very dangerous to say that God had a special purpose for the pandemic. A pandemic is an epidemic that can affect anyone. Therefore, when talking about God's will through the pandemic, we could easily misunderstand it as God's warning to all of mankind.

Ji-sun Lee, author of *I Love You, Ji-sun*, who suffered a full body burn, and YouTuber Park Wi (Weracle channel), who was paralyzed in the lower body, both confessed they did not want to go back to the way they were before their accidents. The lessons they learned were that precious. However, we cannot generalize these terrible accidents themselves as a channel of God's grace.

In many cases, God's will is revealed through extremely personal enlightenment. If the pandemic is understood as God's revelation, its destructive nature itself becomes an "aggressive revelation." The Holocaust or a tsunami demonstrates the same reason these are not God's "revelations. Kate Bowler titled her book this way: *Everything Happens for a Reason and Other Lies I've Loved*. To tell someone who is battling a disease (and at their most vulnerable point in life) that there is a reason for their disease can be the most "brutal aggression," the author says. I have made this mistake in the past. In legalistic faith, everything is read as part of God's will. We often forget that having "compassion" for a suffering person is God's will in and of itself.

Let us imagine a scenario in which the pandemic was, in fact, a "revelation of God": What did God want to say? I can think of two things. One is the idea that the pandemic is a punishment for those who had turned away from God. But Jesus taught us to repent of our sins every day and to pray for the Kingdom of God to come on earth. Repentance is not achieved because a disease has befallen mankind.

Crying with the Pandemic 2

Matthew 21:33–39 tells the story of the parable of the tenants. It is an absurd story of tenant farmers who, instead of taking care of the owner's share when he was away, killed all the servants sent by the owner—and even his son, the heir of the owner. In this story, the son of the heir represents Jesus. N.T. Wright, in his book *God and the Pandemic*, says the heart of this story is that Jesus is the only "last messenger" of repentance and judgment sent to us.

Another is the idea of viewing the pandemic as a "cornerstone of revival." Of course, God can cause a greater revival through a pandemic. However, the view that God purposely allowed the pandemic in order to produce a revival is similar to interpreting that God caused the Korean War for the revival of South Korea or allowed the Holocaust in order to establish the State of Israel.

Therefore, it is important to consider in what nuance and in what context the terms *revelation* or *God's will* are used. I like the saying, "Nuance is everything." The will of God is usually not known right in the moment. In many cases, it is found retrospectively. And in many more cases, you might never know all the answers.

I want to interpret the pandemic in the frame of both "mourning" and "hope." Knowing that this world is not the end, I live with the "hope" of the future resurrection. However, just as a newborn cries, I also "mourn" with those who are suffering from disease and pain. The Jesus of hope, who gives life to the dead man Lazarus, also mourns with those who loved Lazarus. Anxiety and hope cannot coexist. But sadness and hope can. Anxiety cannot be hopeful because an anxious person cannot trust or rely on anyone. However, even in the midst of our grief, we can speak of hope because we rely on

God. Jesus said, "Blessed are those who mourn, for they will be comforted" (Matthew 5:4 NIV).

Faith is an attitude, not an inner skill. The more you build up your inner strength, the higher you can go and the more you become a "mentally tough cookie." Unlike inner strength, faith becomes more humble over time. It is about imitating the greatest humiliation, of Jesus' coming down to earth as a human being. I once believed that if my faith deepened, I would walk and run and fly away. I thought that when I reached a certain level, I would not see most hardships as hardships, and I would always be able to rejoice in the Gospel. But now I confess that faith is about holding Jesus' hand and walking, or even crawling with Him. It is grace that makes it possible to cry and walk with Jesus.

Wouldn't God be most pleased with me if I shared the pain with my cancer patients as well as the people in my community and around the world suffering from COVID-19? I, too, am comforted and strengthened by Jesus, who sympathizes with my pain. However, I often forget the tears of the Lord, who is crying because of the sickness and suffering of my neighbors. Shouldn't we go beyond the grace of "God shares my pain" and move on to "I share His pain"? Now is the time to go from "praying while looking at the sky from the ground" to "praying in mourning while looking at the ground from the sky."

In Jonah 1:2, God told Jonah, "Arise, go to Nineveh, that great city, and cry against it" (KJV). God grieved for the 120,000 people of Nineveh who fell into sin. He wanted

Jonah to cry out in sorrow, as well. Of course, Jonah did not rejoice at the repentance of Nineveh, Israel's enemy. Jonah was not interested in the salvation of the people of Nineveh. Rather, his interest lay in the gourd vine; he became enraged when this vine, which had provided him with cool shade, withered and died. This reminds me of myself when I could not stand the little discomforts in my life while ignoring the immense suffering of others. Curiously, the book of Jonah does not end with a confession of repentance like the book of Job. Meeting my Nineveh with "God's mourning" is the way to complete the book of Jonah. The creative musical *Jonah*, performed at the Sight & Sound Theater in Pennsylvania, ends with Jonah accepting God's kind of "mourning" as his own and crying together with Him. In this sense, mourning provides an escape from self-centeredness.

When there was a great famine in Jerusalem, the church in Antioch helped the church in Jerusalem (Acts 11:28–30). As Tom Wright pointed out, in this context, the Church focused on who needed help, what help to send, and to whom send it, rather than seeking God's will for the famine and the reason behind it. Likewise, during the pandemic, wouldn't it be a more biblical response to identify who is at the highest risk for suffering during this epidemic, what specific help we can give, and how we can share the words of warm encouragement and comfort?

I learn a great deal from the nurses at our cancer clinic. Even when everyone was exhausted due to the pandemic, to celebrate the day one of my patients reached a meaningful treatment milestone without experiencing any side effects, our team made a handwritten certificate and held an award ceremony, sincerely rejoicing with the patient. One patient who was filled with the dream of spending her last wedding anniversary at Disney World was depressed that she had no choice but to cancel her trip due to COVID-19. Our nurses then decorated the chemotherapy room with Disney World photos to celebrate her wedding anniversary together.

Could a life of mourning but gaining strength in hope be called a "bipolar life"? The Bible verse that tells us to "rejoice with those who rejoice, and weep with those who weep" (Romans 12:15 NKJV) refers to a life in which the words of Romans 12 become flesh. It is a life of rejoicing when someone is cured as if it were my own recovery and mourning in the face of pain and death as if it were my own suffering. I wish to pass through the pandemic era with both sorrow and hope.

"I Will Be with You until the End"

Hope for Finishing the Race

As the phrase "battling a disease" implies, many people see cancer as an enemy. In a fight, there are always winners and losers. It is a framework that says "either I win or cancer wins." According to this analogy, death means "losing the battle" against cancer. However, even if it is not cancer, our lives will come to an end—whether it is due to an accident, another disease, or simply old age. Cancer is only a small part of our long lives.

That is why I prefer to see the "marathon" as a metaphor for life. If life is a marathon, then the last moment of your life is the day you finish the marathon. Of course, the length and difficulty of each race varies. Nonetheless, everyone eventually completes the course, no matter what type of chemotherapy they endure.

Can I Pray for You?

It is not a bad thing to use a battle metaphor for cancer research. The name of the cancer research building at Seoul National University College of Medicine, my alma mater, is *Jeong Bok-dong*, which literally translates to "building of conquest." It is true that cancer is a disease that must be conquered through research. In the battle against cancer, we are winning small-scale battles through advances in different areas such as immunotherapy and personalized therapy. I think of my life as a cancer researcher as my life as a commander leading this battle. Every time I see small victories, I feel joy and reward.

I often say to my students that the "patient never fails." This is because in the hospital, we often use the expression that the "patient failed" the treatment. The more precise expression is that the cancer in the patient's body has failed to respond to treatment. If the medical staff and patients use the expression "the patient who failed in treatment" frequently, they are both bound to fall into a defeatist mindset. No, the patient is just passing through difficult courses in the marathon of healing.

As a doctor, it is unfortunate that I cannot always guarantee the best results, but I can support my patients by running alongside them at every mile of the journey. Therefore, my concluding words of every first meeting with a patient are always the following: "The road may be bumpy, but I will work very closely with you." I tell them I cannot guarantee that they will not have any difficulties but that I will be with them.

"I Will Be with You until the End"

In his book *Reuniting Church*, Pastor Young Ho Park suggests that when proposing to a woman, a man should say, "I'll never let you cry alone," instead of "I'll never let you cry." He is a good husband even if he can cry with his wife when she is hurt. Likewise, if you have a good family and medical staff who warmly support you when you are exhausted from the difficult journey of treatment, couldn't the marathon turn into something beautiful?

If You Know the Thrill of the Countdown

Even today, I often recall the words Dr. Soo-hyeon Ahn told his leukemia patient in his book, *That Young Foolish Doctor*:

> "It is God who will heal you. What I pray for is not for you to be cured, but for me to perform your song given by the Lord as best as I can and then go off the stage with thunderous applause from the saints and angels."

When I complete the journey of life, which was given to me as a gift, what will I look like? My emotions can fluctuate with each treatment result, but wouldn't it be important to prepare for my death by imagining the last moments of my life? While asking for a miracle is a worthy prayer, there were no miracles on the cross, and so I want to focus on Jesus, who will bring me back to life, not my body, which will perish. It can be sad to us here on the earth when miracles don't happen. One caregiver responded to my request to pray for the patient by saying, "Please give her practical help rather than a prayer." I think about how difficult things were for him and sad he must have been.

Jesus must have been sad on the last day of His life, as well. His disciples had betrayed Him. They left Him and watched from afar, but no one came to help Him. He asked God, His Father, to take away His suffering, but God was silent. Jesus was whipped and had no energy to carry the cross. But Jesus focused on the reason He had come to this earth: to forgive our sins and to give us eternal life. He knew best that He had to fulfill His mission of death on the cross.

Perhaps Jesus overcame the sadness and climbed the hill of Golgotha, where the cross awaited, with excitement. His work culminated at the cross. The countdown to the moment on the cross had begun. It was time for Jesus to make His final spurt in the race of His life, a moment of glory to fulfill the purpose for which He had been born.

I hope that I can feel the excitement of that countdown in the last moment of my life. I want to cross the finish line with excitement, fulfilling at last the mission God has given me for my life. I pray that my patients also complete their lives in such a beautiful way.

To cheer and congratulate the patients who are struggling on this road to completion, my team members and I make awards for them. In order to establish a *culture* of encouragement, rather than having it be a *onetime* event, I started the "Pacemaker Movement," which continues to this day (www.pacemakerstogether.org). As the name of this

"I Will Be with You until the End"

movement implies, I want to be a pacemaker for my patients and be with them so they can run at their usual pace in the marathon called chemotherapy.

As part of this movement, we interview patients, their family, their friends, and the medical staff, and we share their valuable stories on the YouTube channel (my pacemaker interview video QR code). We create a certificate for those who are still on the difficult treatment journey to support them to the completion of their treatment.

One day, a patient who was undergoing chemotherapy for malignant mesothelioma came in with a bright smile on her face. I asked if something good was going on. She told me she had been thinking about her funeral a lot lately, because her death might not be far off. Initially, she said she was upset that she would not meet the guests who would need to travel far to attend her funeral. The guests would gather to remember her and talk about her in her absence. Soon, she changed her mind and came up with a new idea: She sent out invitations to a "funeral eve" party to all her loved ones as if she were prepping for the funeral. The party would not be a "funeral to mourn" her death, but instead a "party of life" to rejoice and celebrate that she had lived well and was still alive on that day.

My conversation with her made me realize the importance of rejoicing in the present (now) as a present (gift) given to us. It reminded me of the words of the Bible: "Death was swallowed up by life" (see 2 Corinthians 5:4). Living today as if it were eternity, instead of shifting our focus to the new life given after the death of our body, would be the most beautiful way of running the marathon of life.

Pacemaker

by
Young Kwang Chae

How tough it must have been
What a challenging situation
I know you didn't wish for this
I understand

How tough it must have been
How your disappointment must have been
The pain of the circumstances
I cannot even imagine
How tough it must have been

Are you eating well?
Are you sleeping well?
Can you breathe well?

How tough it must have been
Due to the uncertainty,
The unpredictable path to recovery,
The worry of being a burden to others

Rest assured
I will be your pacemaker till the end
I will run with you
I will walk with you

Your marathon
Is my marathon.

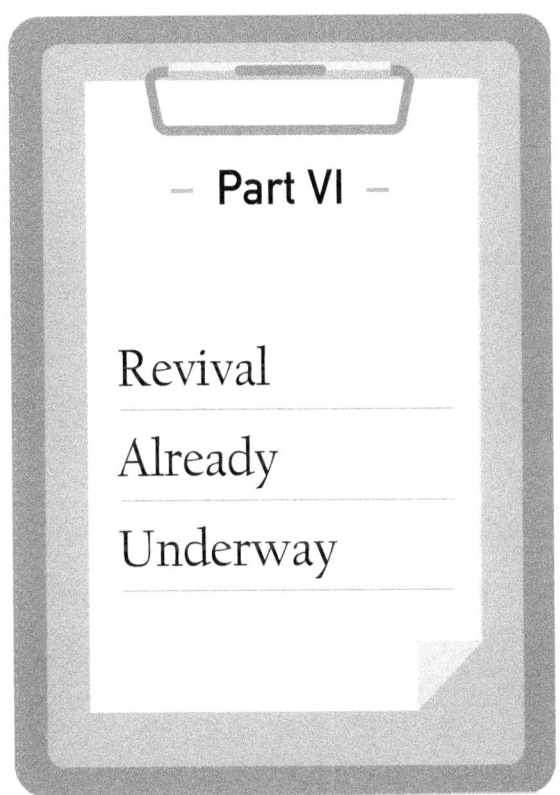

Part VI

Revival
Already
Underway

One Who Heals Friendships

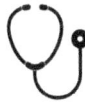

Depart from Me

As I began to love God, my sins became more apparent in my eyes. I saw the end of myself. When sins I didn't even know existed came to mind, it was truly agonizing. Before the faultless God, my existence felt infinitely small. Just as the lyrics of the song "Love" say, "Why do I become smaller when I stand in front of you?" it's normal to feel humble in front of the one you love. How much more so in front of God? When the Holy Spirit illuminates my conscience, I feel completely naked.

This feeling is well-expressed in the words of the Bible: "When my soul was embittered, when I was pricked in heart, I was brutish and ignorant; I was like a beast toward you" (Psalm 73:21–22 ESV). Daniel's words to God, "O my lord, by reason of the vision pains have come upon me, and I retain no strength" (Daniel 10:16 ESV), also echo a similar context. Similarly, Peter's response to Jesus' words, when he obeyed and his boat was filled with fish, shows an unexpected reaction. Instead of asking Jesus to stay with him, he humbled himself under Jesus' feet, saying, "Depart from me, Lord, for I am a sinful man" (Luke 5:8 JUB). Could it be that Peter was expressing the sentiment of "You are too much for me," as opposed to "Go away from me"?

I enjoyed watching the Korean drama *Because This Is My First Life*. Ji-ho, the female lead, enters into a contract marriage with the male lead, Seahee, solely to save on rent. However, later on, she develops genuine feelings for Seahee. Eventually, Ji-ho informs Se-hee that she intends to end the marriage. Because their marriage didn't start with true love, Ji-ho paradoxically tells Se-hee, "You are too much for me now, so please leave me."

My relationship with God might not be so dissimilar to theirs. At first, I approached God with impure motives, asking God to do this or that, as if He owed me these things. However, when I started to love God with all my heart, I began to think, *I do not deserve God's grace instead.* Psalm 8:4 asks the question, "What is man that you are mindful of him, and the son of man that you care for him?" (ESV), speaking of this undeserved grace given to those who do not deserve it.

If I stand before God without humility making me infinitely small, reminding me that I am "poor in spirit," then I have no hope. Before I had this mindset, I had a habit of comparing myself. I would feel conceited when I saw someone less accomplished than me, and I would feel down when I saw someone more successful.

One Who Heals Friendships

Behind these comparisons was "self-love." When I felt inferior and discouraged in comparison to those more capable than me, and when I felt superior and proud when comparing myself to those less accomplished, the focus was solely on myself. Whether consciously or unconsciously, I judged others and myself by the standards I set for myself. I thought, *I should be treated to this level,* or, *I should have at least this much.* I was upset when my expectations were not met.

My conceit stemmed from considering myself better than others in certain aspects. When I reached a certain level, I believed I should enjoy certain privileges, that the world shouldn't treat me unfairly, that I should receive recognition from others, and that I should be acknowledged for my hard work. I was living within the self-centered framework I had established.

Loving oneself more than God—the Bible labels this as a sin. It's self-idolatry. I came to realize that I needed to repent of this sin. The only path to becoming whole is to be crucified with Christ and to die on the cross. A dead body does not get excited. A dead body does not get wounded. The Bible testifies that the more people love themselves, the more they distance themselves from God. The more important I become, the less room there is for Jesus. He becomes diminished. The treasure inside the jar of clay, the light of Christ, fades away.

I now dream of a "Christ-centered" life, rather than an "I-centered" Life. As long as my ego exists, there is no place for the dreams of Christ. When I reflect on my wounded heart, all that remains is depression and despair. Therefore, I want to focus on solving others' problems instead of obsessing over my own. I've abandoned the idea of studying or earning money to serve later. A life serving God and my neighbors is an ongoing progress in my church, school, and workplace.

Nick Vujicic, author of *Hug: Life without Limits*, confesses that he couldn't help but feel despair in the face of his congenital limblessness. However, he also testifies to living joyfully today through the grace he encountered in that situation. In the moment I recognize that the hardships I've endured can be part of God's plan, that His sovereign power is at work in my difficulties, I no longer see my wounds, but instead I see Christ. Henri Nouwen calls people who help others through their own sufferings "wounded healers."

I refuse any more self-pity. I also reject cynicism. I rise with a broken heart. I don't rely on people; I rely only on God. I don't place my hopes in people; rather, I serve them as I serve the Lord.

The term *light pollution* refers to the presence of excessive light from the buildings in the city that makes it difficult to see the stars in the night sky. I ask myself if the spotlights in my heart are only illuminating the various shapes of my wounds. Now I'm extinguishing these spotlights one by one. It's then that Christ, who should truly shine, is revealed in the light.

One Who Heals Friendships

God Is My Friend

Among the books by C.S. Lewis that I admire is *The Four Loves*. I even chose this book for my book club at one point. In *The Four Loves*, Lewis divides love into four different types: affection, friendship, eros, and charity. There's a particular story in the chapter about "Friendship" in this book that stands out. C.S. Lewis and J.R.R. Tolkien, the author of *The Lord of the Rings*, were members of a literary club called the Inklings. A friend named Charles Williams was also part of this club, and Lewis uses the relationships among these three individuals to illustrate the attributes of friendship. Lewis once mentioned that only Williams's jokes could evoke genuine laughter from Tolkien. However, when Williams passed away from cancer, Lewis sadly recalls, Tolkien's laughter, too, faded away.

Friendship is finding joy in the company of friends and delighting in each other's qualities that can only be experienced when together, as opposed to interactions with those who aren't friends. In friendship, there's a generosity that surpasses mere mutual affection, which can be observed in romantic relationships. I contemplate how blessed it is to have friends who bring out the best in me, even parts I didn't know existed within myself, and to share companionship with them.

What's remarkable is that God considers *us* as *His* friends. In John 15:15 (NIV), Jesus says, "I have called you friends, for everything that I learned from my Father I have made known to you." In Luke 12:4 (NIV), Jesus starts His teachings with "My friends," and in Exodus 33:11, God's interaction with Moses is described thusly: "The Lord would speak to Moses face to face, as one speaks to a friend" (NIV).

We encounter God based on our character and experiences, which is why the way we experience God's presence and image differs from person to person. God has made each of us unique and has allowed us to experience Him in unique ways. He brings out the best in us, even the things we could not see ourselves. His Grand Plan works differently for us because the plan is specific to each of our lives. Just as Lewis enjoyed seeing Tolkien laughing at Williams's jokes, we gain so much joy sharing our experiences with God and discovering His vast and multifaceted character.

The Bible repeatedly advises us to come together and encourage one another. It is through our fellow communities that we come to know God our Friend more deeply and discover the beauty of other human friendships. As we hear the astonishing stories of God working in the lives of our brothers and sisters, we are moved by His keen insight, His gentle whisper, His detailed guidance, His steadfast love, and His unfailing compassion; the heart of the Lord who never abandons us, who shares in our pain and touches us deeply.

We often wonder, *Does God love others more than me?* In these moments of questioning, though God may not answer directly, witnessing the abundant testimonies of answered prayers from others can lead us to feel as if God loves them more. It's during times like these that we might feel excluded from the waterfall of God's grace, like we are wandering through a spiritual desert, feeling jealous of my friend's successes.

The author of *Letting Go,* missionary Yongkyu Lee, shared the book and spread God's love through his ministry, yet paradoxically without noticing his wife falling into depression. Similarly, there are moments when the gracious testimonies of others do not resonate as grace for us. Even during conversations with friends, there are times when listening to their stories at length about their glowing successes can at some point make them sound cocky and annoying.

Perhaps what is important to remember in moments like this is that our beloved Friend, God, is our God and our friend. Even when we can't see God's work in our own lives right now, if we see a new aspect of God's work in the lives of our brothers and sisters beside us, we might exclaim, "Wow, my God has done such amazing things! Our incredible God!" How wonderful would that be?

Here, let's reconsider the attribute of "Friendship" among *The Four Loves*. I think about how great it is not only to have my own God, but to share the same God with my family and friends. Rather than feeling uncomfortable when sharing God with others, if we can be thankful that it's not just my God but our God, then every day filled with others' successes and celebrations will be joyous and heartwarming. In a similar vein, isn't it wonderful having siblings because we can experience and appreciate our parents together, despite our differences? Likewise, we hope that the joy of sharing God together will never fade. Moreover, taking a step further, how wonderful would it be if we could hold the expectation that our God, who works marvelously in the lives of our brothers and sisters, can also work in our own lives in His desired time and way, creating something even more magnificent? Just as friends consider one another, we contemplate our Friend, the infinitely attentive God who cares for us. Before we open the door of our hearts, we think of our God, who quietly knocks and waits outside. The Lord has said: "Here I am! I stand at the door and knock. If anyone hears my voice and opens the door, I will come in and eat with that person, and they with me" (Revelation 3:20 NIV).

Reflecting on Jesus Christ, our Friend, who desires to share all our secrets with us, as we approach God's love through the keyword *friendship*, as described by Lewis, we experience the grace of encountering Him afresh and anew today.

Living Like I'm the Last Christian

The One Person He Is Looking For

It does not take too many people for a wound to heal and for a relationship to recover; one person is enough. When treating cancer patients, I often encounter rude patients or their caregivers. Some individuals, amidst life-threatening situations, displace that stress onto the medical staff.

Once, the granddaughter of a Caucasian patient bombarded me with several impolite questions. Such incidents, when they recur, make me weary as well, seeing as I am also human. However, during the next consultation, this grandmother looked into my eyes and apologized.

Surprised and clueless, I asked her, "What's wrong?"

She said, "I was so upset that my daughter was being so disrespectful. I apologize from the bottom of my heart."

"Don't worry, I'm okay," I answered.

Can I Pray for You?

"I don't feel okay," she said. "This shouldn't have happened. I apologize on her behalf. Please forgive us." Watching her speaking with tears in her eyes, I could feel her sincerity.

I had actually met so many rude patients that I thought I had some immunity by that time. Yet, a sense of self-disgust and bitterness remained within me. However, meeting this grandmother led to the forgiveness of all rude incidents, not only involving her granddaughter, but also with all other patients. My difficult emotions melted away like snow. Paradoxically, I felt more openhearted toward the patients. Through this incident, I realized the power of "apologizing on behalf of, seeking forgiveness on behalf of." I discovered that healing requires the sincerity of just one person.

There is a story about Kwang-sik Park, a saxophonist, after his concert in Japan. An elderly Japanese woman from the audience approached him and apologized as if she were apologizing for all the wrongdoings of Japan to Korea. Although she wasn't the prime minister or the minister of defense, her genuine apology moved Kwang-sik Park profoundly. From then on, after each concert, Park gave the following apology at the end of each concert:

> "I'm a Christian. I would like to take this opportunity to apologize on behalf of all Christians for disrespecting you and hurting your feelings."

I believe the process of recovering broken relationships begins with a humble and sincere apology from one person who has set aside his or her pride. The Bible also speaks of

Jesus as the prime example of forgiveness. Jesus alone took on the sins of the world and sacrificed Himself so that our relationship with God could be reconciled.

There were times when I thought, *This is a person whom the Lord seeks.* I also want to be such a person, especially since most of my patients are nearing the end of their lives. I wish to fulfill the role of a "Christian who meets them in their last moments."

As part of my mission, I would also like to use this space to say to patients suffering from all kinds of illnesses, including cancer, and their caregivers: "If you have been hurt by the words or actions of rude or indifferent medical staff, I genuinely apologize on behalf of all medical staff. Your feelings are valid. I humbly ask for your forgiveness."

One Jewish elderly patient with advanced lung cancer, undergoing chemotherapy, expressed gratitude to me whenever we met. She asked me to convey her gratitude to my mother, who had given birth to me. I faithfully relayed her words to my mother in Korea. My mother was deeply moved. I also experienced something special. Her sincere gratitude was evident in her eyes and voice, even causing my eyes to well up. Finding the source of existence and expressing gratitude is truly beautiful. I believe that through my service, the God who is the Source of my existence receives that gratitude, which contributes to a life that brings glory to God. Just as one person who genuinely seeks forgiveness can lead to reconciliation, one person who genuinely expresses gratitude, like me, may be the person the Lord seeks.

Can I Pray for You?

Patients often express their gratitude in cards or letters, including cancer patients who are suffering from chemotherapy and surgery. Reading a thank-you letter from a patient with advanced lung cancer who successfully completed chemotherapy and surgery recently made me reflect on the power of gratitude. His letter made me once again stand in awe of God. Through me, someone insignificant, producing gratitude in life, I found myself thinking more about the "Owner of Gratitude," God:

> "After receiving treatment last Monday and leaving your clinic, I was in shock and unable to fully accept the fact that the cancer was gone. My heart was all tangled up because I had never heard of anyone's cancer going away so quickly. You probably thought that I was the most ungrateful person in the world because I wasn't running around, shouting how grateful I am for this. Six hours after leaving the office, I have finally come to accept this unbelievable news, and I am now writing this letter to you. I don't know how to express my gratitude to you and your team for planning a treatment plan that allowed me to become cancer-free. You are truly miracle-workers. I've been keeping the fact that I had cancer a secret, but now it's gone! It saved my sister from months of worrying about me. Let me know if you ever need me to be a witness to the amazing things your team is doing. I will always be here. If you had told me nine months ago that I would be cancer-free by September, I probably wouldn't have believed it. Thank you so much for saving my life."

The Blessing of Bahurim

There were times when I was subjected to absurd attacks in hospitals and universities; those attacks came from fellow doctors, students, and nurses. There were other times when my good intentions were misunderstood; in those moments, I felt helpless and resentful at the injustice of a false accusation. I often felt like I was trying to recover from a hard blow to my head. Once, when I was feeling dizzy and numb, I had a sudden thought: *Could the One who permits this situation be God? If so, what kind of response does God want from me?*

I wanted to firmly suppress them, so that they would never treat me in such a way again. However, the thought that they were also precious children of God, like me, who were redeemed by the precious life of Jesus, came to mind.

Therefore, I resolved to endure only for the sake of Jesus. Just as Jesus would have done, I decided to wait for them.

Bahurim is the place where King David meets Shimei while fleeing from his son Absalom, who is trying to kill his own father (2 Samuel 16:5-13). Shimei throws stones at David and cusses him out mercilessly. He mocks David's pitiful plight and curses that God is punishing a murderer like David as he deserves. At that moment, David's loyal general, Abishai, wanted to kill Shimei, but David restrained him, saying: "If the Lord has told him to curse me, who are you to stop him? . . . And perhaps the Lord will see that I am being wronged and will bless me because of these curses today" (2 Samuel 16:10 NLT).

Afterward, when King David and his followers crossed the Jordan River and took a rest there, they regained their strength. Scripture records that through this rest, David and his people recovered. I believe that David's attitude displayed in Bahurim, where he endured curses despite his innocence, was one of the reasons God later exalted David. Judgment is not my responsibility but solely God's. I can only take refuge in the One who is my sole refuge. God exalted David again through the process of Bahurim. This is the blessing that comes through passing through Bahurim.

When passing through Bahurim, when we were still sinners—that is, when we had no insight into the sin of leaving God—we remember Jesus, who died for us. There is no use trying to see through the psychology of those who attack us. When Jesus was crucified, he begged God, "Forgive them, for they do not know what they are doing" (Luke 23:34 NIV). Secular psychology may advise cutting ties with such individuals. However, Jesus asked if He could sacrifice Himself for them even when they might not know what they are doing wrong. He asked if one could still embrace with love and wait with faith. Thus, now I endured my Bahurim period by solely focusing on Jesus. I can confess that it was a time of proud blessings before the Lord when I could stand and say it was a time when I thought only of Jesus.

"Blessed are you when people insult you, persecute you and falsely say all kinds of evil against you because of me.

Rejoice and be glad, because great is your reward in heaven, for in the same way they persecuted the prophets who were before you" (Matthew 5:11–12 NIV).

Keyword 10

Obedience: the spiritual Ohm's law

Every morning, I feel a sense of urgency that I must crucify my selfish ego on the cross. This is because I earnestly desire to live with the reality of "it is no longer I who live, but Christ lives in me" (Galatians 2:20 NKJV). Christian rapper Lecrae expresses it this way:

> "Each morning I have to attend a funeral—my own. I have to wake up and once again die to my desires for people's approval."

The funeral represents a ceremony where the desire for people's approval is buried, and the desire to conform to the world's values of competition is discarded.

The less ego I have, the less resistance that holds me back and the more I can see God working through us. I would like to call this phenomenon the "Spiritual Law of Ohm." In physics, Ohm's law states, "I (current) = V (voltage) / R (resistance)," showing that the current is proportional to voltage and inversely proportional to resistance. If God's infinite power is the voltage, then the resistance can be considered my self-esteem, pride, and sin. The current is the flow of life

Keyword 10

and the Holy Spirit's interaction. The voltage comes from the high heavenly throne, from the humble manger, and from the cross on Golgotha Hill.

Although the voltage is infinite, the current of life cannot flow if my ego is still alive. The switch that lowers this resistance is none other than prayer. Therefore, I consider prayer as the practice of dying, just like Jesus. Becoming like Jesus means reducing the resistance to "0." When I die and become poor in spirit, I see the work of Jesus within me. Even if circumstances do not change, the life of Jesus is manifested in our bodies.

"We are hard pressed on every side, but not crushed; perplexed, but not in despair; persecuted, but not abandoned; struck down, but not destroyed. We always carry around in our body the death of Jesus, so that the life of Jesus may also be revealed in our body" (2 Corinthians 4:8–10 NIV).

This is the life I do not desire, yet I confess. In the eyes of the world, it might seem like there is nothing left, like I am being beaten here and there. However, because Jesus' life is in the place where I have died, I can walk with the Lord today.

In Luke 5, Jesus told Simon Peter, who had worked all night without catching any fish, "Put out into deep water, and let down the nets for a catch" (Luke 5:4 NIV). By obeying this word, the nets were so full of fish that they began to break. In contrast, in John 21, after the resurrection, Jesus appeared to Simon Peter, who had caught no fish the previous day, and told him, "Throw your net on the right side of the boat and

Keyword 10

you will find some" (John 21:6 NIV). This time, the net was full, but it did not break.

What is most interesting to me is that the net is torn at first, but not when Simon Peter encountered the resurrected Lord. The "net," which is both a tool and my ego, must be torn for the Lord to enter me. However, like Peter, once we have experienced the net being torn and then recognize and walk with the resurrected Lord, our net will no longer tear. In our life's place, the "net" given to us, namely our abilities or talents, will be used to circulate the blessings of the Lord.

The Beginning of Mission

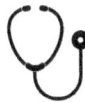

Overcoming the Logic of Cost-effectiveness

One of the things medical trainees like to discuss with their colleagues is the number of patients they see: "There's always someone on call who gets a lot more patients than other on-call physicians working on the same floor. That physician has to stay wide awake because patients get admitted all throughout the night. Meanwhile, the few lucky ones get zero patients, so they sleep comfortably all night in the call-room."

In Korea, a resident who often has to handle a high number of patients during their shift is humorously referred to as a *hwan-ta*, meaning "ridden by patients." In the United States, they call it "black cloud." With the same salary and the same training, any physician would gladly choose to be in a place where the workload is relatively manageable. However, I felt uncomfortable with this topic being the most interesting part of their discussions; some colleagues would even feel embarrassed because they saw so many patients while others would boast that they saw fewer patients.

In contrast to the structured training period with fixed income, when one starts a practice, they seek to attract as many patients as possible with minimal effort. I also considered the concept of "cost-effectiveness" to be of utmost importance; achieving the greatest outcome with the least effort and cost. If the structure makes it difficult to achieve significantly better results, then I was interested in how one could pursue a better quality of life (QoL) within that framework. I was curious about what specialty could provide such conditions and what workplace would allow for this. Indeed, many doctors, including myself, have a motive to practice medicine in the United States, as they feel this environment provides more opportunities to fulfill these desires.

However, as my faith grew, I found myself less interested in cost-effectiveness. I realized that true liberation from cost-effectiveness marks the beginning of my mission. Often, when we experience God supplying our needs in unexpected ways and at unexpected times, the formula for cost-effectiveness in which we had initially believed loses its significance. More than success or failure, what became important was simply carrying out my mission. As I began to serve others and make that a priority ahead of my own success, I developed a faith that God would take responsibility for my success. I learned that even if I do not gain recognition or wealth in the world, as long as God approves, it is more than enough.

I frequently ask myself why I became a doctor and why I am doing what I am doing now. Especially when I read

The Beginning of Mission

personal statements or write recommendation letters for my students applying to medical school or residency, I pay close attention to how they answer these questions. None of them mention cost-effectiveness in these formal writings. Many times, I'm touched and happy to discover their sincere intentions. While hoping for their sincerity, I also advise myself to return to my own initial motivations.

I pray to God to love patients with a humble heart, to rejoice in their recovery together, to feel their sorrow deeply, and to overcome the logic of "cost-effectiveness" with my "first heart." I pray to turn the worldly "cost-effectiveness" into a sacred "extravagance." I have composed a poem titled "Extravagance," which encapsulates my heart.

Extravagance

by
Young Kwang Chae

Knowing the cost, I cannot waste
Considering time, I cannot waste
Taking out the calculator, I cannot waste

So I practice extravagance
Not asking for value
Not thinking of time
Not calculating

So I practice love
Spreading with joy
Giving without holding back
Apologizing for not giving more

Embracing the wicked poverty
Welcoming it like a guest
Like the fragrance of a broken alabaster flask
Believing that extravagance will save my love

The Beginning of Mission

I sought mentors closely from school and work, longing for continuous role models. But I later realized that it was more important for me to become that kind of mentor for my own disciples, my mentees. I mentored them so they, in turn, could become precious mentors for their own disciples. The fact that I could be the start of this chain reaction fills my heart with joy. How I can love patients more, teaching the mentors of the future this, will benefit their patients and their disciples. Yes, I take pride in being a mentor who serves the mentors of the future.

Looking back, I realize my true mentor is Jesus. I draw inspiration from His flawless character and endless love. Every morning, I seek His wisdom and practice script reading, acting out scenes from my life under His direction—the Writer and Director of my life.

Likewise, my campus ministry is a "cameo ministry." I receive my script from Jesus and make guest appearances in my disciples' lives. When my role is finished, I leave the stage. Sometimes, while mentoring, discomfort creeps into my heart. Reflecting on this discomfort, I realize I've wondered in the past, *Does this friend see me as insignificant?* I've even pondered whether my mentees, who request seemingly unreasonable things from me, find me easy to exploit. At times, I've questioned whether I'm making myself too accessible. But as long as I faithfully play my part according to the Director's cues, I know I'll be fine. The desire has arisen in me to see my disciples excel beyond me. When my role fades away, it's a proud moment to say that they've done better than me. There are times when my mentees can only see the sacrifices they have made; but rather than judging them, I want to become a doctor and a researcher who can see the bigger picture.

If you look through the eyes of an expert, you can immediately get the quotation value of a candidate; whether the candidate has any potential becomes very clear. A quick glance at the résumé and a few words exchanged in an interview give you a good sense of the kind of potential a candidate has. There have been times when I was tempted to tell my mentee that it would be better to give up; I wanted to tell my mentee that he or she was hopeless with only that much ability.

However, there is something I have definitely given up on: standing in God's place, judging and evaluating others in God's place, and refusing to stop until God tells me to stop. Now I believe that even people who seem inadequate in my eyes can be used wondrously if God so decides. In fact, God does not use people with qualities that appear outstanding by the world's standards. Rather, He usually makes use of people who are unsuccessful and inexperienced. So I tell the mentors of the future: treat everyone like someone who will surely succeed; some people are late bloomers, waiting for their time to shine.

"God chose the lowly things of this world and the despised things—and the things that are not—to nullify the things that are" (1 Corinthians 1:28 NIV).

Go and Do Likewise

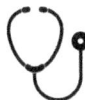

There Are Moments That Change Lives

The story of the Good Samaritan (Luke 10:30-37) serves as a typical model of Christian mission. The story begins with a Jewish man traveling from Jerusalem to Jericho. He encounters a robber on the way and is attacked, robbed, and left injured. Both a priest and a Levite pass by the wounded man without helping. However, the Samaritan, despised by the Jews, comes to his aid. Jesus uses this story to ask who the true neighbor is, the one who shows mercy when it's difficult.

Whether in a mission field or our workplace, we can reflect on what we need to live out this story. The priest and the Levite passed by the wounded man without helping. They might have been busy with their duties, or they might have disliked Samaritans. But the despised Samaritan couldn't simply pass by a dying man. Something within him compelled him to help. The Bible simply says that the Samaritan "saw him [and] had compassion on him" (Luke 10:33 KJV). The Samaritan listens to his inner voice that tells him he should help the injured man more than anything else. Rather than thinking that others might help, he feels a strong sense of calling to help this person.

David is another biblical figure who, while listening to his inner voice, walks up to the front of the battlefield and takes revenge on Goliath for insulting God. Jesus, too, could not let any merchants disturb the Temple of God, His house of prayer. Pastor Everett Swanson decided to establish an international child-rearing organization called Compassion in 1952 after seeing the body of an orphan dumped in a trashcan during the Korean War; the organization is now active in twenty-five countries. Father Tae-seok Lee devoted his life as a missionary to South Sudan, where he could not walk past people suffering from poverty and disease.

There are moments when we hear a life-changing calling from the Lord. It's like Popeye eating spinach to rescue Olive, transforming him. It's when you become a true missionary proclaiming God's Kingdom where it doesn't exist. At work, when you feel that you cannot leave a dying patient in the intensive care unit without teaching him the Gospel, you have embarked on your own missional journey. If you want to encourage and comfort the patient's family with the Gospel, the bedside visit can turn into a medical mission field. For Dr. Soohyun Ahn, the hospital was the mission field itself. Medical missions begin when you align your heart with God's. Once my heart aligned with His, I had many moments when I cried with my patients.

Go and Do Likewise

However, mere intentions alone are not enough to fulfill God's mission; You need to sacrifice your body, resources, and time. If you're wondering whether you'll be compensated for the time and money invested, it's better not to help at all. But if you're determined to help, true dedication means doing your best within whatever is your capacity to assist.

The Bible records that the Samaritan "went to him and bandaged his wounds, pouring on oil and wine. Then he put the man on his own donkey, brought him to an inn and took care of him" (Luke 10:34 NIV). Sacrificing his time and resources, helping without seeking personal gain, this Samaritan becomes the true role model for missionaries.

Lastly, this story makes us think about the sustainability of medical missions. The Bible says, "The next day he took out two denarii and gave them to the innkeeper. 'Look after him,' he said, 'and when I return, I will reimburse you for any extra expense you may have'" (Luke 10:35 NIV). Medical mission is a commitment to continuous service; it is not about helping once and forgetting afterward. Just as the Lord tells Peter three times consecutively to shepherd His sheep, a medical mission is like shepherding; no message will be delivered without consistent, persistent follow-up. Whether you meet a child on a mission field or a patient admitted to the ward, you must continuously pour your time and energy into serving. God's love is the driving force of medical missions; our duty is to help people experience His enduring love.

Can I Pray for You?

You Become a Neighbor When You Do the Work Yourself

A short-term medical mission participant once said that her missionary work felt futile; she prescribed medications with no guarantee that patients would adhere to the medication protocol and comply with follow-up. Even those who participate yearly felt like they were only providing a onetime assistance each year. There are many modes of missionary work, and there is no single answer. Chun-Sun Choi, known as the "Barefoot Angel," said, "Missions are individual, but loyalty yields fruit." I believe that God was praised through it all—visiting areas where doctors are a rare sight, showing the locals a gesture of love, and embracing them through prayer.

Just as businesses within a company have different departments, and just as different ministries exist within a church, medical missions also come in various forms. In places where there are no surgeons available, there are individuals who perform surgeries and procedures even without proper facilities. Some go as far as performing spinal surgeries. Some people collect surplus medical supplies and equipment and donate reusable resources to developing countries. Others are dedicated to nurturing local medical talent by establishing medical schools and nursing colleges in mission fields. There are also those who dedicate themselves to preventive care, education, and long-term health screening in mission areas. During my time studying at the Johns Hopkins Bloomberg School of Public Health, many individuals devoted themselves to these tasks. Some were interested in raising up local experts, as part of their belief in the value of community empowerment. Deciding which type of Christian ministry is more important and which is less important is as impractical as trying to put a price on life itself.

Dr. Alfred Sommer, the former dean of the Bloomberg School of Public Health, demonstrated through randomized clinical trials that when children in third-world countries take vitamin A twice a year, their annual mortality rate decreases by 34 percent. This is because children with vitamin A deficiency have weaker immune systems, resulting in a higher risk of death from infectious diseases. Sommer's project has been cited as the most cost-effective and life-saving medical project ever, along with the mosquito net supply project in malaria-prone areas. At the other end of the spectrum, funding bone-marrow transplants for relapsed acute leukemia patients, despite costing millions and offering no guaranteed success, might appear wasteful. However, both these endeavors are valuable in the eyes of God, and it's important to serve with a heart that judges each situation according to His will.

In medical missions, there is no hierarchy or greater or lesser importance of a task. During my three years of public health work, I often traveled by boat to provide health care in remote islands where seasonal winds carry disease, including Pungdo and Yukdo, on the west coast, almost every month for three years. I traveled with volunteer hairdressers every time. Their dedication was truly admirable. Similarly, beauticians often work alongside medical mission teams in different areas. If you ever find yourself believing that medical missions are more important than beauty services, it's a moment to reflect and repent.

Let us go back to the parable of the Good Samaritan. At the end of the story, the Bible reads: "Which of these three do you think was the neighbor of the robber?" Jesus asks, and the lawyer answers, "The one who showed him mercy." Then Jesus says to him, "Go and do likewise" (Luke 10:36–37 NIV). The story of the Good Samaritan mainly centers on the answer that Jesus gives when the lawyer asks, "Who is our neighbor?" (verse 29 NIV).

In reality, Jesus never explicitly labeled the Samaritan as "good" in this story. It's just that over time, people began to refer to this story as the parable of the "Good Samaritan." The point is not to live as kindly as the Samaritan did. Jesus is not describing that person as good or even explaining the concept of being a neighbor. He commands us to do exactly that—help those in need, care for those who require healing, and look after them just as we would our own family members.

However, there's a secret here. When we help in that way, we can experience the true joy of being a true neighbor, a true child of God. The Samaritan could have ignored the dying Jewish man, who was despised and treated as an enemy. But he set aside such feelings and cared for him as he would for his own family member, nursing him back to health. Jesus' command for us to do the same is because in order to truly live as neighbors, we must help in that way. When the Samaritan saved the dying Jewish man, he was able to forgive and love the Jew who had initially harbored ill feelings toward

Go and Do Likewise

him. It might seem like the message is "help the sick when you are healthy," but it's actually "help others recover so that you yourself can experience spiritual revival."

In fact, all of Jesus' commands ultimately serve our own benefit. Many individuals who engage in missions have shared how they went to offer blessings, but they ended up receiving the most blessings themselves; "I went to give," they say, "but I received too much." Jesus says that if we are determined to give, we will live. A mission is ultimately God's calling and blessing for us to live an abundant life in Christ.

Another important point is that the Samaritan didn't find a reason to help the wounded man himself. He didn't analyze whether or not the man was worthy of help or deserving of it. If he did, he would have had ample reasons to walk away from a seemingly hopeless situation. Instead, he focused on being in a position to help through the health and resources God had provided him.

Likewise, the reason to care for a patient doesn't come from the patient themselves. They might not understand your words, and they might frustrate you. They might ask questions even after working hours are over. The reason to help shouldn't be sought in the attitude of the patient. Similar to the Samaritan, you must find it simply in the fact that you are in a position to help at that moment.

We ourselves can become the "man who fell into the hands of robbers" at any point in our lives. Those who serve in disability ministries say that we ourselves or our family members could become disabled at any moment. Thus, helping the disabled is a ministry that ultimately helps ourselves in the future. Perhaps the Samaritan in the Bible might have had a warm memory of someone who helped him when he was injured. This paradigm shift changed the nature of missions. Missions are not a matter of choice. Living on a mission is a command from the Lord to save myself and my neighbors who have been robbed or who may be robbed in the future.

Dreaming of the Grapevine Ministry

Gentle Waves of Revival

Our lab alumni often mention that they felt a strong desire for the first time to spread the Word of God more than they had ever wanted to before. Some people who move to other states say they go with the heart of being sent as missionaries. I can feel that a tidal wave of revival has begun in our little lab here in Chicago.

There are three principles in medical education: see one, do one, teach one. Similarly, here in our lab, we bring about change by observing, doing for, and encouraging one another with sincere love, prayers, and consideration for each other and for the patients. I share every aspect of my daily life, clinical work, research, and prayer life with my disciples, as if I am being filmed in a documentary. Just as missionaries experience change when they live with the natives, I also witness my mentees' lives changing. I imagine my mentees working in every part of the world and nurturing other disciples. I dream that they become seeds of revival, spreading God's love. Just imagining it fills me with awe, as the Cambridge revival also started among seven students in England at the end of the nineteenth century.

In the past, revival felt like a huge, unapproachable concept to me. However, I now believe this could simply be witnessing God's sovereign, ongoing work. All I need to do for a revival to happen is create a space where people can encounter God. The work of spinning the wheel is done by God. We, unqualified individuals, only need to stand in that privileged place of undeserving grace. We simply need to be the bridge between God and our neighbors. It is a ministry in which I make enough space for the Lord to complete the work He has started.

Poet Jeong-rok Lee said this in his poem "Chair": "Both the flower and the fruit, that's all there is / Just sitting in a chair. Living isn't any different / Putting a few chairs in a good, shady place with nice scenery." Could the revival of God also happen when we offer the chair?

Giving It a Name: Grapevine Ministry

As I was writing this book, I thought of how great it would be if the ministry in Chicago could spread to more clinics and labs. As I prayed for the book I was writing with the heart of a debtor, it felt as though God's heart was given to me.

Dreaming of the Grapevine Ministry

The idea of writing a book started when missionary Taehoon Kim invited a publisher to a Zoom meeting where I was giving a testimony about my ministry. I was not aware that the publisher had joined our meeting. To the publisher, my ministry reminded her of the work of God in the Acts of the Apostles. She reached out to me privately afterward, encouraging me to write a book about my ministry, as it is not something that can be imitated. However, now I no longer wanted my ministry to be unique and exclusive; I started writing with the hope that any mentors could imitate my ministry.

Therefore, instead of calling it the Chae Lab Ministry, I wanted to give it a new name to signify that it is a ministry led by Jesus Himself. I desired that my name disappear and only reveal the name of Jesus. "He must become greater; I must become less" (John 3:30 NIV).

With the help of my disciples and fellow mentors, we voted to choose a name for this ministry, and it was given the name Grapevine Ministry. Jesus said, "I am the vine; you are the branches. If you remain in me and I in you, you will bear much fruit; apart from me you can do nothing" (John 15:5 NIV).

The name of this ministry has five meanings. Firstly, Jesus, who represents the vine, is our only Source of life. This means that it is not my ministry, nor the ministry of other mentors, but it's solely the ministry of Jesus.

Secondly, we are just branches; we just pave the way for others. We cannot do anything without the vine; especially in the case of grapevines, the branches are useless as wood. Only the tree that is valued by its fruit is a grapevine. Without being attached to Jesus, we are nothing. Conversely, by staying attached to Him, we receive everything. Thus, the core of this ministry is to just remain in that position. Then, you will receive blessing by witnessing the Lord's provision.

Thirdly, we rely on God, our farmer. As Jesus became the vine, He also depended on God the Father. Likewise, at any moment, we acknowledge and revere God.

Fourthly, the fruit of the vine is not a grape, but another vine. The only way to grow another vine is for my ego (the grape seed) to die and for Jesus (the vine) to live in me (Galatians 2:20). It's about disciples becoming teachers and those teachers raising disciples again.

Lastly, it's about becoming friends with Jesus. Friends, not servants, have no secrets. Jesus shared everything He learned from the Father with us (John 15:15). The vine has nothing to hide from its branches; it provides everything generously. This ministry is about the vine and branches working together as friends and bearing fruits together. It goes further, becoming friends with patients and disciples. Jesus says, "Greater love has no one than this: to lay down one's life for one's friends" (John 15:13 NIV). This ministry is about serving patients and disciples by dying to self, laying down stubbornness and pride, serving coworkers in faith like friends, encouraging patients like friends, and comforting their families. I dream that this ministry, now named the Grapevine Ministry, will spread throughout the world like wildfire.

Dreaming of the Grapevine Ministry

To express the spirit of the Grapevine Ministry, I created a song with my students in the research lab. The title is "Standing in That Place" (lyrics by Sally Jung and Young Kwang Chae, composed by Sally Jung). The lyrics progress as follows: "Father, pour Your love on me/ Let Your Kingdom come into my heart/ You who suffer with troubled souls/ Lord of life, I rely on You today.// Father, pour Your mercy on me/ Let Your words fill my heart/ Lord, You suffer through pain with me/ Lord of life, I rely on You today.// Lord, when You pour Your heart on one soul/ We will stand where there is healing and recovery/ We are Your faithful servants; You guide every step we take/ Through us, Your image will be restored/ Your Kingdom will come/ We will stand where we belong."

I wholeheartedly believe that whatever happens, God will accomplish it in His time and His way. Setting specific goals and strategies often leads to excessive impatience and pressure. I prayed to God that I wanted to express my heart through music and lyrics. It was an astonishing prayer from me, since I have never composed a song before.

Thankfully, with the help of my students' support, His grace to create the second song for the Grapevine Ministry, entitled "It Will Be Fulfilled" (lyrics and music by Young Kwang Chae), was granted. These two songs have been uploaded on the Grapevine Ministry YouTube channel.

The lyrics go like this: "Turn your gaze away from what you lack/ Look at what the Lord has prepared for you/ Encounter the God who delights in you/ Rest comfortably in His vast embrace// If you have Jesus, you have everything/

When His time comes, He will fulfill/ Not in your time, but His/ In the name of Jesus, nothing is impossible/ Only through His Word, He will fulfill/ You will fulfill// Even if you can't see ahead in the darkness/ Be thankful for everything the Lord has given you/ Meet the joyful God who calls you/ Find peace in the living Lord/ If you have Jesus, you have everything/ When His time comes, He will fulfill/ Not in your time, but His/ In the name of Jesus, nothing is impossible/ Only through love, He will fulfill/ You will fulfill."

Epilogue
Dreaming of a Strange Vineyard

I went on a medical mission trip to Mexico with my daughter. On my second day there, I was asked to give a testimony. Although my body was sore from the first day's schedule, my heart was pounding with excitement. What stories should I share? I picked one without hesitation during the bumpy ride back to my hostel on the outskirts of the city. It was the parable of a vineyard in Matthew 20, which I shared earlier. I suggested to the college students who came with me that we should live like vineyard owners.

As I conclude this book, I reflect on my current activities and realize that my place of service, my mission field, is, indeed, this vineyard. After two years, what I'm doing in my research lab and in my medical practice is aligned with the work of a vineyard owner. What was especially comforting to know was that the owner truly enjoyed his job. For him, serving his vineyard workers was more important than producing grapes. I was certain that God was pleased with the vineyard.

My vineyard, which operated differently from the ways of the world, felt like an ideal place where God's will was being done. My clinic and my lab might become known as "Chicago's strange vineyard."

When the Samaritan woman meets Jesus at the well, she recognizes that Jesus is her Messiah. She is so overwhelmingly happy that she leaves the water jar and runs back to the village to tell everyone about Jesus. The story does not end there; the townspeople came to Jesus themselves. They invited Him to their homes, listened to His words, and told the woman, "We no longer believe just because of what you said; now we have heard for ourselves, and we know that this man really is the Savior of the world" (John 4:42 NIV).

My role is no different from the Samaritan woman at the well. It is to testify joyfully through this book that Jesus is my Savior. However, there might be some who perceive my story as unrelated to them and close the door of their hearts even more tightly. Even worse, there may be some who feel even more depressed or sad after reading my book. For those who are worn out by the world and have hardened hearts, the success stories of others can become wounds. Nevertheless, the God I testify about is the God of us all. My desire is to proudly share the goodness and faithfulness of our God. It's like discovering the good deeds my father did secretly and later realizing and proudly proclaiming, "Our Father is the best!"

I would like to give my readers my warmest blessings. I hope you immerse yourself in His words, just as the villagers

Epilogue: Dreaming of a Strange Vineyard

did by inviting Jesus to give a talk. May we all be able to dream of the day when we can share in God's life. Just like rowers in a boat look back and keep rowing, my life seems to be similar. I see only the past events. The river we've already crossed is visible, and I faintly glimpse the waves of grace that God has shown. Looking back, I don't know what course lies ahead of me. I can only speculate that there might be more unexpected courses and megaton-level trials waiting. Nonetheless, I believe that if I follow Jesus, who knows all my future from the helm of my boat, even death will be transformed into life. Even if my plans crumble, I believe that God's purpose for me will be fulfilled.

"In their hearts humans plan their course, but the Lord establishes their steps." (Proverbs 16:9 NIV).

As I close this book, I leave you with the words I tell my patients who defy the odds: you are stronger than you know, and hope always has the final word. And the God who began His work in you will surely finish it, beautifully.

It's a Miracle

(Young Kwang Chae)

I am a doctor, yet still, I declare—
A miracle is a miracle, rare.

That breath by breath, through joy and strife,
You've held on tight, still filled with life.

That every step, though worn and weak,
Has led you here—no small feat.

That though your tears fall, one by one,
You speak of hope when day is done.

So let me say, with reverence true,
A miracle stands here—in you.

You are, to me,
A miracle indeed.

About the Author

Dr. Young Kwang Chae is a husband of a lovely wife who led him to Christ. He is a loving father of three children. He is a compassionate oncologist who specializes in treating cancers refractory to standard of care therapies. After graduating from Seoul National University College of Medicine, he completed his Master's Degree in Public Health (MPH) and Business Administration (MBA) at Johns Hopkins University. He did his residency in internal medicine at the Albert Einstein Medical Center in Philadelphia, then proceeded to pursue fellowship in hematology and oncology at The University of Texas MD Anderson Cancer Center in Houston. Dr. Chae is currently a full professor of Northwestern University Feinberg School of Medicine, treating cancer patients, teaching residents, and leading pioneering research projects. He is the vice-chair of the Early Therapeutics and Rare Cancers Committee of the US Clinical Trials Group, SWOG, where he plans and organizes clinical trials on a national scale with the U.S. National Cancer Institute (NCI). Dr. Chae was awarded the NCI Director's Award for his leadership and his contribution in innovative cancer research.

"May I come in?" A simple greeting opens up the room, as Dr. Chae walks in with a big smile lighting up his face. Walking alongside his patient, he speaks resilience and hope during the difficult cancer treatment journey under the grace of God.

Since 2009, he has served as a lecturer and a coordinator for the KOSTA medical seminar in the U.S., and a mentor for Global Medical Missions Alliance (GMMA), a medical missions organization. In addition, he holds seminars in various organizations for cancer patients and their families to spread the importance and the need for faith. He is a leading mentor of the Grapevine Ministry, established in Chicago in 2021, and is a founding mentor of the Pacemakers movement.

You may contact the author at

branch.grapevine@gmail.com

www.ingramcontent.com/pod-product-compliance
Lightning Source LLC
Chambersburg PA
CBHW072151070526
44585CB00015B/1097